Pittsburgh Series in Bibliography

Pittsburgh Series in Bibliography

HART CRANE: A DESCRIPTIVE BIBLIOGRAPHY
Joseph Schwartz and Robert C. Schweik

HART CRANE

Portrait of Hart Crane by David Siqueiros

Hart Crane

A DESCRIPTIVE BIBLIOGRAPHY

Joseph Schwartz *and*
Robert C. Schweik

UNIVERSITY OF
PITTSBURGH PRESS

Library of Congress Catalog Card Number 73-151508
ISBN 0-8229-3228-8
Copyright © 1972, University of Pittsburgh Press
All rights reserved
Henry M. Snyder & Co., Inc., London
Manufactured in the United States of America

For Joan and Joanne

Contents

Illustrations

Acknowledgments

IN the preparation of this bibliography we have had the kind assistance of many individuals and institutions—of many more, in fact, than it is possible for us to thank individually. We wish, however, to express our gratitude to the members of the Editorial Board of the Pittsburgh Series in Bibliography, Fredson Bowers, William Cagle, Charles Mann, and especially Matthew Bruccoli, and to Mrs. Louise Craft of the University of Pittsburgh Press, who was editor of this volume. In addition, we wish to acknowledge special debts of gratitude to Joseph Katz, Kenneth Lohf, Allen Tate, John Unterecker, and Brom Weber for generous assistance. It is a pleasure to express our appreciation to our colleagues Clifford Helbert and Strother B. Purdy of Marquette University and Douglas Shepard of the State University of New York for their knowledgeable advice and assistance. We wish, also, to thank the following individuals who have provided important help in various ways: Miss Elizabeth Devine and Rev. John Talmage of Marquette University Library; Hugh C. Atkinson of the Ohio State University Libraries; William Bonellie of Smithers & Bonellie, Ltd.; E. A. Digard of the Guernsey Press Co., Ltd.; D. D. Ginsmore of William Young & Co.; K. C. Gay, Curator of the poetry collection of the State University of New York at Buffalo; Betty Godfrey of Thomas Nelson & Sons; Pyke Johnson, Jr., of Doubleday Anchor Books; Harlan Kessel of the University of California Press; Thomas H. Nichols of the U.S. Copyright Office, Robert H.

Land of the Library of Congress; Julius Lewis of
the Van Rees Press; Arthur Pell of the Liveright
Publishing Corp.; Laurence H. Scott of the Massachusetts Institute of Technology; and Jon Stall-
worthy of Oxford University Press. We are grateful
to our research assistants F. Peter Ott, Kevin Harty,
and especially William Graczyk. Of the more than
fifty libraries whose collections we have used in
preparation of this bibliography, those to which we
owe special debts all have deen identified in one or
more of the various lists of copies examined which
we have provided elsewhere in this volume; here
we have only the pleasant duty of conveying to
them our special thanks. We are especially grateful
to the Committee on Research at Marquette University for its support of one of the authors with
research funds and a Faculty Fellowship.

*   *   *   *   *   *   *   *

Grateful acknowledgment is made to the following for permission to reproduce material in this
book: Columbia University Library, for the portrait
of Crane by Siqueiros; Leonard Baskin and The
Museum of Modern Art, for the title page from A 8;
Doubleday & Company, Inc., for the title pages
from A 9 and A 10.1; Liveright Publishing Corporation, New York, for title pages from A 1.1, A 1.2,
A 3.1, A 3.3, A 4.1, A 4.2, A 4.4, and A 10.2 and the
illustration of p. 48 from A 3.1, all from the works
of Hart Crane; Kenneth A. Lohf, for the title page
from A 11 and the broadside, A 12, which is repro-
duced also by permission of the artist, Laurence H.
Scott; David Mann, for "Annunciations" from *The
Pagan,* "C33" from *Bruno's Weekly,* and Crane's
drawing of Slater Brown from *The Dial;* The Ohio
State University Libraries, for the title page from
A 13 (Copyright 1968, The Ohio State University

Libraries, All Rights Reserved); Oxford University
Press, for the title page from A 10.3; Brom Weber
(title pages from A 7.1, A 7.2, and A 10.2 and the
illustration of p. 294 from A 7.1 from Brom Weber,
ed., *The Letters of Hart Crane, 1916–1932* [1952;
1965], copyright 1952 by Brom Weber, by permission of Brom Weber).

Photographs of the illustrations have been provided by the repositories housing the originals as
follows: A 1.1 (p. 2): Courtesy of the Rare Book
Room, Buffalo and Erie County Public Library;
A 1.1 (p. 5), A 2, A 3.1, A 4.2, A 5, A 6, A 7.1, A 10.2,
A 10.3: Courtesy of the Poetry Collection, Lockwood Memorial Library, State University of New
York at Buffalo; A 1.2: Courtesy of the New York
Public Library; A 3.3, A 4.4, A 7.2, A 13: Courtesy
of the Library, State University of New York, College at Fredonia; A 4.1: Courtesy of the University
of Chicago Libraries; Frontispiece, A 12: Courtesy
of Columbia University Library.

Introduction

ALTHOUGH Hart Crane's status as a major twentieth-century poet is now firmly established, there has been no complete descriptive bibliography of his works available. Students of Crane owe an important debt of gratitude to Kenneth Lohf for the meticulous care with which he prepared his bibliography of Crane's manuscripts,[1] but, unfortunately, Crane's printed works have fared less well. Two years after Crane's death, John Birss prepared a short bibliographic note which provided an incomplete listing of Crane's works,[2] and in 1936 another brief listing was compiled by Merle Johnson.[3] More recently, Brom Weber has provided important bibliographical information in his edition of *The Complete Poems and Selected Letters and Prose of Hart Crane*,[4] but not, of course, the material of a descriptive bibliography. And from time to time other bits of bibliographic information on Crane's works have been published in various places. For anyone seeking the information provided by a descriptive bibliography, however, the only available source has been the inac-

1. Kenneth A. Lohf, ed., *The Literary Manuscripts of Hart Crane* (Columbus: Ohio State University Press, 1967).

2. "American First Editions: (Harold) Hart Crane (1899–1932)," *Publishers' Weekly*, 125 (June 16, 1934), 22–23.

3. *American First Editions: Bibliographic Checklists of the Works of 199 American Authors*, 3rd ed., rev. Jacob Blanck (New York: R. R. Bowker, 1936).

4. Brom Weber, ed., *The Complete Poems and Selected Letters and Prose of Hart Crane* (New York: Liveright Publishing Corp., 1966).

curate and incomplete *Hart Crane: A Bibliography,*
compiled by H. D. Rowe in 1955.[5] The present
work, then, is intended to satisfy the need for a full
and accurate descriptive bibliography of Hart
Crane's work.

Our attempt has been to include everything written or drawn by Crane that has appeared in any
published form, including translations and adaptations, excluding only the reprintings of Crane's
works in conventional anthologies published after
1933. Listed first are separate editions arranged
chronologically by initial date of publication and
within each edition chronologically by impressions.
Works not published separately are divided into
poetry, prose, and letters. The poetry and prose are
arranged alphabetically by title, with the history
of the publication of the work and alternate titles
cross-referenced to the main heading. The letters
not published separately are arranged alphabetically by addressee, with the history of the publication of the letter. The drawings of Crane are listed
alphabetically by the subject of the drawing.
Translations of Crane's work are arranged by language and alphabetically by editor, translator, or
title of the work. Adaptations are in alphabetical
order by title. A brief section of doubtful attribu-
tions concludes the bibliography. A more detailed
than usual chronology of Crane's life is included
as Appendix I for the convenience of the users of
this volume. Appendix II provides a chronology of
the publication of Crane's poems, and Appendix III
lists alphabetically the periodicals in which Crane's
poetry and prose first appeared.

The form of entry used for listings in section A is
in general consistent with that recommended in

---

5. *Hart Crane: A Bibliography* (Denver: Alan Swallow,
1955).

Fredson Bowers's *Principles of Bibliographical Description*.[6] Our ordinary procedure has been a sight collation against a control copy of all copies examined. In certain cases (e.g., *Two Letters* published by Jack [John] Birss) a scarcity of copies available made it necessary for a xerox copy to be used in place of a control copy. The following may help to clarify some of the particular practices we have adopted:

Title pages: These have been transcribed in quasi-facsimile form; unless otherwise specified, lettering is solid and in black.

Collations: Collational formulas, statements of signing, leaf number designations, and pagination statements generally follow Greg's formulary as elaborated by Bowers. Inferences are invariably enclosed in square brackets; for pagination, the unnumbered beginnings and endings as well as all internal unnumbered portions of sequences are inferentially noted. Except for cancels, reference to inserted leaves not part of the printed sheets is made neither in the collation note nor in the contents note; such leaves are invariably described separately.

Contents: Quasi-facsimile form has been preferred whenever space limitations permitted. All matter given in quasi-facsimile form is surrounded by single quotation marks; all other quoted matter is indicated by double quotation marks. In cases where we have judged it useful, the bibliographical content note has been supplemented by a literary contents note, included for the convenience of scholars wishing a quick check of the individual

---

6. *Principles of Bibliographical Description* (1949; reprint ed., New York: Russell & Russell, 1962).

titles, prefatory material, and other particulars of
the contents of the volume.

Inserted leaves: Variations in the number, subject, size, and bordering of inserted illustrations
have been noted in detail, particularly as such differences are often related to other differences
between impressions in Crane's work.

Typography: The typography notes ordinarily
supply an identification of the chief typefaces and
typeface sizes used. In the single case of the Paris
edition of *The Bridge,* an extensive search of type-
founders' specimen books has failed to yield an
identification of the typeface, and, therefore, a
detailed description of the face with approxima-
tions of sizes in American points has been substituted.

Papers: Because we found that our own use of
terms such as *creamy white, off-white,* and *gray-
ish white* was not consistent, the term *white* has
been used to include all such variants; only ob-
viously colored paper has been specified as to
shade. Wove and laid papers have been distin-
guished and watermarks noted; measurements of
paper thickness have been supplied.

Bindings: The texture and pattern of cloth bindings have been given in immediately descriptive
terms such as *smooth, diagonal ribbed,* and so
forth, followed by reference in parentheses to the
cloth grain designation symbols such as those used
in Jacob Blanck's *Bibliography of American Literature.*[7] Color in bindings has been indicated in
immediately descriptive terms (e.g., *black, light*

---

7. Jacob Blanck, ed., *Bibliography of American Literature,*
5 vols. (New Haven: Yale University Press, 1955–).

blue).[8] Endpapers have regularly been noted and described. The term *paperback* is used only to signify that type of perfect binding in which a heavy paper wrapping is cut flush and attached by gluing to the spine. The lettering of bindings has invariably been given in quasi-facsimile form. Dust jackets have been described in greater detail than is common and often in quasi-facsimile form; this procedure results not from any overestimation on our part of the importance of dust jacket evidences, but rather from the belief that the description, if provided at all, should be sufficiently precise so as to provide bibliographically useful information.

Notes: Information about the circumstances surrounding the printing and publication of Crane's work has been provided particularly in the case of works published in his lifetime. What printer's copy of Crane's works exists in manuscript form has been described by Kenneth Lohf in his *Literary Manuscripts of Hart Crane;* the nature of printer's copy in other forms has been indicated when that information has been available to us. In the case of books for which copyright applications were filed, we have noted particularly the information such applications provide about the dates of printing and/or publication, as well as the details they supply about the identity of the firms which performed the typesetting, printing,

---

8. The methods of binding description which have been proposed by G. Thomas Tanselle (see Fredson Bowers, ed., *Studies in Bibliography,* vol. 20 [Charlottesville: Bibliographical Society of the University of Virginia, 1963–64] pp. 203–234, and ibid., vol. 23, pp. 71–102) are likely to supplant the relatively less systematic practices like the *BAL* now in common use—especially if they are developed in a handbook for the bibliographic decription of cloth grain and color. At present, however, we do not think them sufficiently well known and/or accepted to be used here.

and binding. Ordinarily we have supplied the names and addresses of these firms; we have indicated whether the printing was done from standing type or from plates; and if printing was done from relief plates of other than cast metal (e.g., rubber or plastic), we have indicated this fact. The testimony provided by copyright applications has been supplemented by information provided by publishers' records; by the dates of accession or cataloguing of copyright deposit copies in America and England; and by the information provided in *Publishers' Weekly, The Bookseller,* and other organs of publishing information. When information about the number of copies printed has been available, this has been supplied.

No attempt has been made to provide a census of Crane holdings, but a list of the locations of those copies examined in public repositories and private collections has been provided for every edition described. Location symbols used are those provided in *Symbols of American Libraries,* 10th edition, published by the Library of Congress Union Catalog Division, 1969. The library of Wisconsin State University at Superior is not included in the Union Catalog list, and we have assigned the symbol *WSupU* to that library; locations of libraries in England are given by their ordinary names. (These location symbols and their definitions are listed at the end of this introduction.) In the "Copies examined" note we have also provided the locations of proof copies, dust jackets, woodcut plates, and copies with special notations when we have had opportunity to examine them. When a copy examined was in some way defective (e.g., with missing leaves or rebound), we have invariably noted the defect; for editions involving two or more states or impressions, we have specified the particular state or impression of each copy located.

Terms: The terms *edition, impression, issue,* and *state* are used in the senses recommended by Fredson Bowers for the description of modern books. With respect to book edges, we have used the term *cut* to refer to edges guillotined, ploughed flush, or fully trimmed so as to leave all edges even; the term *trimmed,* on the other hand, we have reserved for edges achieved by opening the bolts of gatherings while leaving the edge more or less uneven. All type sizes are given in American points; all other measurements are in inches.

We take upon ourselves, of course, responsibility for whatever defects and limitations this bibliography may have. We would greatly appreciate being informed of any errors we have made or facts we have overlooked. Corrections, revisions, and addenda will be incorporated in any subsequent printings of this book.

JOSEPH SCHWARTZ
ROBERT C. SCHWEIK

Location Symbols in Text

HM	Harvard University, Cambridge
IC	Chicago Public Library, Chicago
ICL	Loyola University, Chicago
ICN	Newberry Library, Chicago
ICU	University of Chicago, Chicago
IEN	Northwestern University, Evanston
IU	University of Illinois, Urbana
InNd	University of Notre Dame, South Bend
NAlU	State University of New York at Albany
NBrockU	State University of New York, College at Brockport
NBu	Buffalo and Erie County Public Library, Buffalo
NBuU	State University of New York at Buffalo
NCU	University of North Carolina, Chapel Hill
NFredU	State University of New York, College at Fredonia
NJam	James Prendergast Free Public Library, Jamestown, N.Y.
NN	New York Public Library, New York
NNC	Columbia University, New York
OCl	Cleveland Public Library, Cleveland
OMtsjC	College of Mount St. Joseph-on-the-Ohio, Mount St. Joseph, Ohio
OU	Ohio State University, Columbus
WM	Milwaukee Public Library, Milwaukee
WMM	Marquette University, Milwaukee
WMUW	University of Wisconsin, Milwaukee
WSupU	Wisconsin State University at Superior

A. Separate Publications

White Buildings:
Poems by Hart Crane

With a Foreword by
ALLEN TATE

BONI & LIVERIGHT, 1926

Title page of *White Buildings,* first impression (A 1.1)

A 1 WHITE BUILDINGS

A 1.1
First impression

Title page: White Buildings: | Poems by Hart Crane | *With a Foreword by* | ALLEN TATE | [oval device containing the letters 'B&L' and the silhouette of a monk at a lectern] | BONI & LIVE-RIGHT, 1926

Collation: (7 1/2 × 5 1/16): [unsigned, 1⁸(±1₂) 2–5⁸], 40 leaves, pp. [i–x] xi–xix [xx] [1–2] 3–45 [46–48] 49–58 [59–60].

Contents: p. [i]: 'White Buildings'. p. [ii]: blank. p. [iii]: title page. p. [iv]: '[rule (1 11/16)] | COPYRIGHT 1926 [four dots arranged in a square] BY | BONI & LIVERIGHT, INC. | PRINTED IN THE UNITED STATES [rule (5/8), interrupted by an oval device containing, in white on a black background, the initials 'B&L' and the silhouette of a monk at a lectern, and followed by a rule (11/16)]'. p. [v]: 'To | WALDO FRANK'. p. [vi]: blank. p. [vii]: 'Ce ne peut être que la fin du monde, en avançant. | — RIMBAUD.'. p. [viii]: blank. p. [ix]: 'Certain of these poems have appeared | in the following magazines: *Broom,* | *The Dial, Double Dealer, Fugitive,* | *Little Review, 1924, Poetry, Secession,* | and *The Calendar* (London).'. p. [x]: blank. pp. xi–xviii: foreword by Allen Tate. p. xix: table of contents. p. [xx]: blank. p. [1]: *'White Buildings'*. p. [2]: blank. pp. 3–58: text. pp. [59–60]: blank.

Items included: Foreword by Allen Tate; Legend; Black Tambourine; Emblems of Conduct; My Grandmother's Love Letters; Sunday Morning Apples; Praise for an Urn; Garden Abstract; Stark Major; Chaplinesque; Pastorale; In Shadow; The Fernery; North Labrador; Repose of Rivers; Paraphrase; Possessions; Lachrymae Christi; Passage; The Wine Menagerie; Recitative; For the Marriage of Faustus and Helen; At Melville's Tomb; Voyages, I, II, III, IV, V, VI.

3

Typography: 29 ll., 5 13/16 (5 15/16) × 3 5/16. Text and titles in 12-pt. Caslon Old Face; page numbers in Old Face numerals within brackets centered at the foot of the type page.

Paper: White, laid (chain lines spaced 23/32, running vertically), watermarked with the words 'WARREN'S | OLDE STYLE'. Leaves bulk 1/4; leaf thickness .0059.

Binding: Spine, hinge, and 1/2″ of the board in smooth dark blue cloth; remainder of the board covered with tan paper showing thick dark fibers throughout. Front and back covers: plain. Spine: reading horizontally, all stamped in gilt, at top, 'WHITE | BUILDINGS | [short rule with two diagonal slashes] | HART | CRANE' and, at bottom, 'BONI & | LIVERIGHT'. Top cut; fore-edge and tail trimmed. White, wove, unwatermarked endpapers.

Dust jacket: Dark blue wove paper, with lettering and design in a metallic yellowish white. Front cover: 'WHITE | BUILD-INGS | *by* Hart Crane | [outline of a city skyline] | EUGENE O'NEILL *writes:* | "Hart Crane's poems are profound | and deep-seeking. In them he re- | veals, with a new insight, and unique | power, the mystic undertones of | beauty which move words to express | vision." ' Spine: 'Hart | Crane | [orn.] | [vertically, bottom to top] *White Buildings* | [oval device representing a monk at a lectern] | Boni & | Liveright'. Back cover: oval device containing the letters 'B&L' and the silhouette of a monk at a lectern. Front flap: '$2.00 | HART | CRANE | Hart Crane was born in | Garretsville, Ohio, in 1899. | His academic education was | early broken off, after which | he has been successively | employed as: mechanic, | bench-hand, shipyard bolter- | up, newspaper reporter, hod | carrier, book clerk, shipping clerk, and advertising copy- | writer. | [¶] He has just returned from | the West Indies where he | was engaged in writing a | long poem, "The Bridge." ' Rear flap: advertisement of Ezra Pound's *Personae*.

Notes: Title page cancel.   The title page was originally printed with Allen Tate's first name misspelled as *Allan*. Some copies had been bound and distributed before this error was detected, at which time a cancellans was printed and tipped into the remaining copies. In all other respects the title pages are identical.

Publication.   The first impression of *White Buildings* was published in December 1926 in a printing of 500 copies. This impression was from relief plates made from type set by Van Rees Book Composition Company of 518 Twenty-sixth Street, New York, N.Y.; the printing was completed on December 21, 1926. These plates were used again in the second impression of

White Buildings:
Poems by Hart Crane

With a Foreword by
ALLAN TATE

BONI & LIVERIGHT, 1926

Uncanceled title page of *White Buildings,* first impression, with
Allen Tate's name misspelled (A 1.1)

January 1929. The copyright application for *White Buildings* gives December 28, 1926, as the date of publication and shows the printer to have been Van Rees Press (same address as above) and the binding to have been performed by Van Rees Bindery, 304 Hudson Street, New York, N.Y. Although *Publishers' Weekly* advertised well before the publication date of *White Buildings* that it would be ready in October 1926, there was no advertising near the date of publication itself. The accession date of the Library of Congress copyright deposit copy was January 8, 1927. By April 1, 1929, Liveright reported to Crane that 387 copies had been sold and 121 copies sent out to reviewers. In fact, many of the copies reported sold had been remaindered.

The developments which led to the publication of Crane's first volume were as follows: by 1925 Hart Crane had the manuscript of *White Buildings* ready for publication; he approached Samuel Jacobs, the printer who had done the composition work for E. E. Cummings's *Tulips and Chimneys,* who agreed to publish Crane's manuscript at his own expense at his Polytype Press, 39 West Eighth Street, New York, N.Y. Subsequently Jacobs ran into financial difficulties and told Crane that the manuscript would be better handled by a "regular" publisher; he offered to print the book at a cost estimate of $200.00 for a printing of 500 copies, and suggested that Crane apply to Harcourt, Brace. Crane submitted his manuscript first to Thomas Seltzer and then to Harcourt, but it was rejected in July 1925. Waldo Frank then brought it to the attention of Boni & Liveright, who tentatively agreed to publish the book if Eugene O'Neill would write a foreword.[1] Although there is some confusion about this matter, Crane apparently was convinced that O'Neill had agreed to these terms, and in March 1926 Crane sent "a hasty bundle of notes" which seem to have been written at O'Neill's request for suggestions as to what approaches he might take to Crane's poetry. From the subsequent correspondence of Waldo Frank, Eugene O'Neill, and Crane, it appears that by May of 1926 O'Neill gave evidence of being unable to complete the foreword. In June, Liveright decided that he would not publish the poems, and Susan Jenkins Brown reports that he said that "he didn't care for the poems and as far as he could see, nobody understood them." At this point, James Light, the theatrical director, and Eugene O'Neill came to Crane's aid: they both

1. An account of Crane's relations with the Liveright firm is provided on pages 129-133 of Walker Gilmer's *Horace Liveright: Publisher of the Twenties* (New York: David Lewis, 1970).

told Liveright that they thought he should publish the poems even if he himself did not care for them, and Liveright again agreed to do so if O'Neill would write a foreword. Allen Tate then volunteered to write an introduction which could be published under O'Neill's name if necessary. Eventually, Tate's introduction appeared under his own name, and Liveright had to be satisfied with a dust jacket blurb by O'Neill.

Text.   Of the poems which went to make up the text of *White Buildings,* only four had not been previously published in magazines: "Emblems of Conduct," "The Fernery," "Sunday Morning Apples," and "Voyages IV."

A 1.2
Second impression: A second impression of 250 copies of *White Buildings* was printed in 1929, differing in the following ways from the first:

Title page: White Buildings: | Poems by Hart Crane | *With a Foreword by* | Allen Tate | [oval device containing the initials 'HL' and the silhouette of a monk at a lectern] | HORACE LIVERIGHT, 1926

Contents: p. [iv] was adjusted to indicate the difference in the firm name and to record the fact of the second impression; it reads, '[rule (1 11/16)] | COPYRIGHT 1926 [four dots arranged in a square] BY | HORACE LIVERIGHT · INC | [rule (1 11/16)] |*Printed in the United States* | [double rule (5/8) interrupted by an oval device containing the initials 'HL' and the silhouette of a monk at a lectern, followed by a double rule (5/8)] | First Printing, January, 1927 | Second Printing, September, 1929'.

Paper: White, laid (chain lines spaced 1 11/16, running vertically), watermarked with an oval device containing the initials 'HL' and the outline of a monk at a lectern. Leaves bulk 1/4; leaf thickness .0063.

Dust jacket: As for the first impression, except for changes made on the spine and front flap.[1] Spine, all reading horizontally,

---

1. The comment by Eugene O'Neill which had appeared on the front cover of the dust jacket used for the first impression was used again on the dust jacket of the second impression. The account of the printing of the O'Neill quotation supplied by Susan Jenkins Brown ["Hart Crane: The End of the Harvest," *The Southern Review,* 4 (Autumn 1968), 978] is inaccurate on this point, as well as incomplete in the quotation supplied from the dust jacket.

OCl: 811.5/C8497w (first impression with cancellans title page)

OCl: 252/C539 (first impression with cancellans title page)

WM: 811/C8917 (first impression with cancellans title page, rebound)

A 2 THE BRIDGE
First edition

Holland paper issue

Title page: [in red] THE BRIDGE | A POEM | by | [in red]
HART CRANE | *With Three Photographs* | *by* | *WALKER EVANS*
| The Black Sun Press | [in red] Rue Cardinale | [in red] Paris
| MCMXXX

Collation: (10 5/8 × 8 5/8): [unsigned, 1-12⁴ 13⁶], 54 leaves,
pp. [1-108].

Contents: pp. [1-4]: blank. p. [5]: 'THE BRIDGE | From going
to and fro in the earth, | and from walking up and down in it. |
The Book of Job.' p. [6]: blank. p. [7]: title page. p. [8]: blank.
p. [9]: '*This First Edition of The Bridge* | *is gratefully dedi-
cated by the author* | *to* | *Otto H. Kahn*'. p. [10]: blank. p. [11]:
table of contents. p. [12]: blank. p. [13]: '[in red] TO BROOK-
LYN BRIDGE' followed by text. p. [15]: 'I | [in red] *AVE MARIA*
| Venient annis saecula seris, | Quibus Oceanus vincula rerum |
Laxet et ingens pateat tellus | Tethysque novos detegat orbes
| Nec sit terris ultima Thule. | *Seneca*.' p. [16]: blank. pp. [17-
21]: text of "Ave Maria." p. [22]: blank. p. [23]: 'II | [in red]
POWHATAN'S DAUGHTER "—Pocahuntus, a well-featured but
wanton | yong girle . . . of the age of eleven or | twelve years,
get the boyes forth with | her into the market place, and make
| them wheele, falling on their hands, | turning their heels up-
wards whom she | would followe, and wheele so herself, | naked
as she was, all the fort over." | 1. The Harbor Dawn | 2. Van
Winkle | 3. The River | 4. The Dance | 5. Indiana'. p. [24]: blank.
pp. [25-48]: text of "Powhatan's Daughter." p. [49]: 'III | [in
red] *CUTTY SARK* | O, the navies old and oaken, | O, the Temer-
aire no more! | *Melville*.' p. [50]: blank. pp. [51-55]: text of
"Cutty Sark." p. [56]: blank. p. [57]: 'IV | [in red] *CAPE HAT-
TERAS* | The seas all crossed, weathered the capes, the voyage
done. | *Walt Whitman*.' p. [58]: blank. pp. [59-68]: text of "Cape
Hatteras." p. [69]: 'V | [in red] *THREE SONGS* | The one Sestos,
the other Abydos hight | *Marlowe*. | 1. Southern Cross | 2. Na-
tional Winter Garden | 3. Virginia'. p. [70]: blank. pp. [71-76]:
text of "Three Songs." p. [77]: 'VI | [in red] *QUAKER HILL* |
I see only the ideal. But no | ideals have ever been fully | suc-
cessful on this earth. | *Isadora Duncan* | The gentian weaves
her fringes, | The maple's loom is red. | *Emily Dickinson*'. p.
[78]: blank. pp. [79-82]: text of "Quaker Hill." p. [83]: 'VII
| [in red] *THE TUNNEL* | To Find the Western path | Right thro'

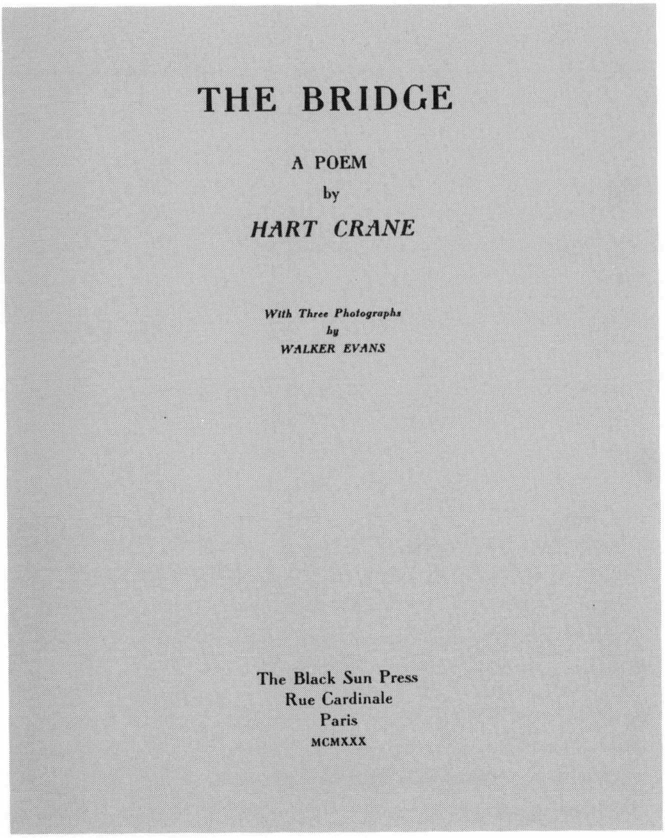

THE BRIDGE

A POEM

by

HART CRANE

With Three Photographs
by
WALKER EVANS

The Black Sun Press
Rue Cardinale
Paris
MCMXXX

Title page of the first edition of *The Bridge*, Holland paper issue (A 2)

the Gates of Wrath | *Blake*.' p. [84]: blank. pp. [85-91]: text of
"The Tunnel." p. [92]: blank. p. [93]: 'VIII | [in red] *ATLANTIS*
| Music is then the knowledge of that | which relates to love in
harmony and system. | *Plato*.' p. [94]: blank. pp. [95-100]: text
of "Atlantis." p. [101]: blank. p. [102]: 'Tous droits de traduction
et de reproduction | réservés par l'auteur pour tous pays'. p. [103]:
'This First Edition of The Bridge by Hart Crane | with three pho-
tographs by Walker Evans | printed for Harry and Caresse Crosby
in | Hand-set Dorique type at their Black Sun | Press, Paris
(Maitre-Imprimeur Lescaret) | in January 1930 is limited to 200
numbered | copies on Holland Paper, 50 numbered copies | on
Japanese Vellum signed by the author, 25 | review copies hors
commerce and 8 special | copies marked A to H. | [space for num-
bering] | For sale at the Bookshop of Harry F. Marks | 31 West
47 Street New York'. p. [104]: advertisement headed, 'Other
Black Sun Publications 1929'. pp. [105-108]: blank.

Illustrations: Three photographs by Walker Evans printed on
three leaves of paper identical with that used for the text. These
leaves were inserted by guarding with sewn wraparound stubs.
Each illustration was covered with a glassine sheet affixed by
wrapping around and gluing along the inner edge of the leaf; a
second glassine sheet was inserted loose between the fixed
glassine sheet and the illustration. The three illustrations are
as follows:
1. glued to a stub sewn with gathering [2], between pp. [12]
   and [13]: recto blank; verso contains a photograph (3 1/8 ×
   1 13/16) of Brooklyn Bridge as seen from below.
2. glued to a stub sewn with gathering [8], between pp. [56]
   and [57]: verso blank; recto contains a photograph (2 11/16
   × 1 5/8) of a tugboat and barges as seen from above.
3. glued to a stub sewn with gathering [13], between pp. [100]
   and [101]: verso blank; the recto contains a photograph
   (2 7/8 × 2 5/16) of Brooklyn Bridge in a perspective showing
   a main pillar as seen through the supporting cables.

Typography: 28 ll., 6 3/16 × 5 7/8. We have been unable to
locate any typefounder's book containing specimens of the
Dorique typeface used to print the Black Sun Press edition of
The Bridge. In a letter to Charlotte Rychtarik dated February
11, 1930, Crane remarked, "The type used is a new French type,
very much like the face which Richard recommended, Gara-
mond." In fact, Dorique is not very much like Garamond: the
nearest approximation we have seen is "Editor Gras" by Fou-
derie Typographique Français, although it is not a particularly
good match. Dorique has the following general characteristics:
an extreme contrast of light and dark elements, as in modern

Romans; some wedge-shaped, bracketed head serifs, rather like late nineteenth-century antiqued Romans; some hairline pedal serifs as in Didot and Bodoni; stress curves irregularly rotated on axis; x-area relatively small, with capitals proportionately tall. The face has three notable idiosyncrasies: uppercase "A" has a cross stroke which extends beyond the left down stroke, and in the italic form this extension ends in a rising ball; uppercase "S" is almost angular because of its tightly accentuated turns, and the top stroke is markedly shorter than the bottom; lowercase "y" has a slightly dented down stroke. The text is in a type size approximately equivalent to a 14-pt. American point system; title on title page in 30-pt. equivalent.

Paper: "Holland paper," a stiff, bulky, white, wove paper. Watermarked with 'VAN GELDER ZONEN'; individual leaves invariably show only a portion of the watermark running parallel with the fore-edge and terminating at the top. Leaves bulk 1/2; leaf thickness .0075.

Binding: Bound by hand, a single stitch (about 5 1/4) through each gathering, the gatherings French sewn, the back unrounded. Top cut; fore-edge, first two leaves of each gathering trimmed, second two untrimmed; tail untrimmed. Covered with a wrapper of stiff, bulky (thickness .0082), white laid paper (chain lines spaced 1 1/8), watermarked with the word 'Arches' and with an 'A' in an elaborate scroll design (the wrappers of some copies examined show no watermark, and, of those examined, only that at the University of Illinois shows the 'A'); the wrapper was glued to the spine, and the front and back covers folded over the top, fore, and bottom edges of the first and last leaves respectively. Wrapper front: '[in red] THE BRIDGE | A POEM | by | [in red] HART CRANE | The Black Sun Press | [in red] Rue Cardinale | [in red] Paris | MCMXXX'. Wrapper spine: letters reading horizontally, words arranged vertically, [in red] 'THE BRIDGE' and 'HART CRANE'; arranged horizontally, '1930'. Wrapper back: on a horizon line, a half-risen sun with seven rays, the entire device in black. The wrapper was covered with a glassine dust jacket, and the whole was enclosed in a cardboard slipcase covered with metallic silver paper. Copies have been seen with other kinds of slipcases—e.g., covered with silver gray cloth, metallic gold paper, and paper designed in blue and white.

Japanese vellum issue
Copies printed on Japanese vellum are identical with those printed on Holland paper except for the following differences:

Contents: p. [103] lacks the lines, 'For sale at the Bookshop of Harry F. Marks | 31 West 47 Street New York'.

Paper: Japanese vellum, a smooth, heavy, brownish white paper, wove and unwatermarked. Leaves bulk 3/8; leaf thickness .006.

Binding: Top cut; tail and fore-edge trimmed.

Review copies
Copies printed for distribution as review copies are identical with those printed on Japanese vellum except for the following differences:

Illustrations: The paper used for the review copy illustrations was Holland paper identical with that used for the Holland paper copies.

Paper: White, laid (chain lines spaced 1 1/16, running vertically), unwatermarked. Leaves bulk 11/32; leaf thickness .0047.

Binding: Top cut; tail and fore-edge trimmed.

Notes to section A 2:   Publication.   Hart Crane met Harry and Caresse Crosby in January of 1929 while on a trip to England and the Continent, and after a first reading of *The Bridge,* they agreed to publish it in a limited first edition at their Black Sun Press in Paris. They urged Crane to remain in Paris in order to finish the poem, and he took up residence in an old mill on the estate of the Compte de la Rochefoucauld at Ermenonville, which the Crosbys had made into a weekend retreat. Crane had promised to complete *The Bridge* before October. When his European sojourn ended disastrously with an imprisonment in Paris, he was given a return ticket by Crosby, who also saw him aboard ship. In spite of his personal difficulties, Crane continued to attempt to keep pace with the printer who started to set the poem in type in August. In order to finish the poem, Crane had still to complete final versions of "Cape Hatteras," "Quaker Hill," and "Indiana." In December of 1929 the Crosbys came to New York for a visit; a few days after Crane had entertained them, Harry Crosby committed suicide. Subsequently Caresse Crosby returned to Paris to see *The Bridge* through the press.[1] The edition consisted of 283 copies. Review copies were

---

1. A brief history of The Black Sun Press has been provided by Milicent Bell, "The Black Sun Press: 1927 to the Present," *Books at Brown,* 17 (1955), 2–24. A description of The Black Sun Press edition of *The Bridge* has appeared in George Robert Minkoff, *A Bibliography of the Black Sun Press* (Great Neck, New York: G. R. Minkoff, 1970). If one

mailed on February 11, 1930, and in the same month copies arrived in New York.

Crane had originally planned additional sections of *The Bridge*, but they were never completed and probably never started: "The Cyder Cask," "The Calgary Express," a Negro Pullman porter's version of the John Brown legend, and a New Year's Eve fantasy called "1927 Whistles."

Illustrations.   Charmion Wiegand had showed Crane a copy of Joseph Stella's monograph, "New York," which contained his painting entitled, "The Bridge." Crane was impressed by this picture of Brooklyn Bridge and wrote to Stella asking permission to use it as a frontispiece to his poem. The Crosbys agreed to use a color reproduction of Stella's picture as a frontispiece and sent to the Brooklyn Art Museum a request to have the Stella picture copied for reproduction; technical difficulties in reproduction could not be overcome, however, and the photographs by Walker Evans were used instead. Crane's interest in the appearance and arrangement of Evans's pictures in the text of *The Bridge* is suggested by his remarks in a letter of December 26, 1929, to Caresse Crosby:

> By the way, will you see that the middle photograph (the one of the barges and tug) goes between the "Cutty Sark" Section and the "Hatteras" Section. That is the "center" of the book, both physically and symbolically. Evans is very anxious, as am I, that no ruling or printing appear on the pages devoted to the reproductions – which is probably your intention anyway.[2]

Numbering and signing.
1. Copies printed on "Holland paper" were numbered on p. [103] by stamping in black ink in the space just above the words, 'For sale at the Bookshop of Harry F. Marks'.
2. Copies printed on "Japanese vellum" were numbered on p. [103] immediately beneath the printed text by stamping in black ink; they were signed by Hart Crane in blue ink immediately beneath the stamped number.
3. Copies printed as review copies were unnumbered and unsigned. The review copy in the Rare Book Room of the New York Public Library has on p. [103] the penciled no-

---

may judge from his account of the paper and contents, Mr. Minkoff seems to have used a review copy impression as the basis of his description.

2. *The Letters of Hart Crane 1916–1932* (New York: Hermitage House, 1952), p. 347.

tation, 'Hors Commerce'; the same penciled notation appears on the review copy in the Harper Library, University of Chicago.

Special copies. We have been unable to locate any of the eight special copies marked 'A' to 'H'.

The English Catalogue listings of Edward Goldston. Edward Goldston was a bookseller whose shop was located at 25 Museum St., London. In 1930 the firm was reorganized as a limited company and subsequently appears listed in *The Reference Catalogue of Current Literature* as publisher of various classes of books, including poetry. The *English Catalogue of Books* for 1930 contains two Goldston listings of *The Bridge*, dated one month apart:

> Crane (Hart)—The Bridge: a poem. 3 photos. by W. Evans. Ltd. ed., 200 nbd. copies. 4to, 42s. net . . . . E. Goldston, Apr. '30
>
> Crane, (Walter)—The Bridge. Ltd. ed., 200 copies. 4to, swd., 42s. net. (Black Sun Pr.) Goldston, May '30

No doubt these two entries refer to the same book, and from the second it seems clear that in this case Goldston intended to act only as distributor for a book appearing under The Black Sun Press imprint. It is not surprising, then, that efforts to locate copies of *The Bridge* bearing the Goldston imprint have been unsuccessful.[3]

Copies examined.
HM: AL 1084.4.30*
ICN: Case/Martin/Y/285/.C8554 (Holland paper)
ICU: PS/3506/.R21B8/1930a (review copy)
IEN: Rare Book Room/LAm/C891br (Holland paper)
IU: Rare Book Room/X 811/ C847b (Holland paper)
NBuU: Poetry Room (Holland paper)
NCU: Rare Book Room/PS3505/R272/B7
NN: *KP/Black Sun/Crane (review copy)
NNC: Special Collections/B812C849/05/1930/copy 1 (Japanese vellum)
NNC: Special Collections/B812C849/05/1930/copy 2 (Holland paper)
OU: Rare Book Room/PS3505/R272B7/1930 (Holland paper)
Oxford University, Bodleian Library: 28121d. 140 (Holland paper)

---

3. See Alan H. Schwartz, "The British Ghost of Crane's *The Bridge*," *American Notes and Queries*, 5 (1967), 150.

Our hearing momentwise; but fast in whirling armatures,
As bright as frogs' eyes, giggling in the girth
Of steely gizzards — axle-bound, confined
In coiled precision, bunched in mutual glee
The bearings glint — O murmurless and shined
In oilrinsed circles of blind ecstasy!

Stars scribble on our eyes the frosty sagas,
The gleaming cantos of unvanquished space...
O sinewy silver biplane, nudging the wind's withers!
There, from Kill Devils Hill at Kitty Hawk
Two brothers in their twinship left the dune;
Warping the gale, the Wright windwrestlers veered
Capeward, then blading the wind's flank, banked and spun
What ciphers risen from prophetic script,
What marathons new-set between the stars!
The soul, by naptha fledged into new reaches
Already knows the closer clasp of Mars, —
New latitudes, unknotting, soon give place
To what fierce schedules, rife of doom apace!

Behold the dragon's covey — amphibian, ubiquitous
To hedge the seaboard, wrap the headland, ride
The blue's unfeathered districts unto æther...
While Iliads glimmer through eyes raised in pride

Page [62] from the first edition of *The Bridge*, Holland paper
issue (A 2)

Stars scribble on our eyes the frosty sagas,
The gleaming cantos of unvanquished space. . .
O sinewy silver biplane, nudging the wind's withers!
There, from Kill Devils Hill at Kitty Hawk
Two brothers in their twinship left the dune;
Warping the gale, the Wright windwrestlers veered
Capeward, then blading the wind's flank, banked and spun
What ciphers risen from prophetic script,
What marathons new-set between the stars!
The soul, by naphtha fledged into new reaches
Already knows the closer clasp of Mars,—
New latitudes, unknotting, soon give place
To what fierce schedules, rife of doom apace!

Behold the dragon's covey — amphibian, ubiquitous
To hedge the seaboard, wrap the headland, ride
The blue's cloud-templed districts unto ether. . .
While Iliads glimmer through eyes raised in pride
Hell's belt springs wider into heaven's plumed side.
O bright circumferences, heights employed to fly
War's fiery kennel masked in downy offings,—
This tournament of space, the threshed and chiselled height,
Is baited by marauding circles, bludgeon flail
Of rancorous grenades whose screaming petals carve us
Wounds that we wrap with theorems sharp as hail!

Wheeled swiftly, wings emerge from larval-silver hangars.
Taut motors surge, space-gnawing, into flight;
Through sparkling visibility, outspread, unsleeping,
Wings clip the last peripheries of light. . .
Tellurian wind-sleuths on dawn patrol,

Page 48 from the second edition of *The Bridge*, first impression
(A 3.1)

A 3 THE BRIDGE
Second edition

A 3.1
First impression

Title page: [within a double-rule frame (external dimensions, 6 3/32 × 3 5/8) enclosed within an ornamental-rule frame of alternating solid squares and spaces (6 7/16 × 3 15/16)] [in red] THE | [in red] BRIDGE | [rule (3 1/2)] | A Poem by | *HART CRANE* | [rule (3 1/2)] | [in red] NEW YORK | [in red] HORACE LIVERIGHT

Collation: (8 5/8 × 6 1/4): [unsigned, 1–5^8 6^4($\pm$6$_1$)], 44 leaves, pp. [i–iv] [1–6] 7–8 [9–10] 11–14 [15–16] 17–35 [36–38] 39–42 [43–44] 45–53 [54–56] 57–62 [63–64] 65–67 [68–70] 71–76 [77–78] 79–82 [83–84].

Contents: pp. [i–ii]: blank. p. [iii]: 'THE BRIDGE'. p. [iv]: blank. p. [1]: title page. p. [2]: 'COPYRIGHT, 1930, BY HORACE LIVERIGHT, INC. | MANUFACTURED IN THE U.S.A.' p. [3]: '*From going to and fro in the earth,* | *and from walking up and down in it.* | THE BOOK OF JOB'. p. [4]: blank. pp. [5–6]: table of contents. p. 7: '*TO* | BROOKLYN BRIDGE | [line of alternating squares and spaces (25/32)]' followed by text. p. 8: text of "To Brooklyn Bridge" continued. p. [9]: 'I | AVE MARIA |*Venient annis, saecula seris,* | *Quibus Oceanus vincula rerum* | *Laxet et ingens pateat tellus* | *Tiphysque novos detegat orbes* | *Nec sit terris ultima Thule.* | –SENECA'. p. [10]: blank. pp. 11–14: text of "Ave Maria." p. [15]: 'II | POWHATAN'S DAUGHTER | "*–Pocahuntus, a well-featured* | *but wanton yong girle* . . . *of the* | *age of eleven or twelve years, get* | *the boyes forth with her into the* | *market place, and make them* | *wheele, falling on their hands,* | *turning their heels upwards, whom* | *she would followe, and wheele so* | *herself, naked as she was, all the* | *fort over.*" ' p. [16]: blank. pp. 17–35: text of "Powhatan's Daughter." p. [36]: blank. p. [37]: 'III | CUTTY SARK | *O, the navies old and oaken,* | *O, the Temeraire no more!* | –MELVILLE'. p. [38]: blank. pp. 39–42: text of "Cutty Sark." p. [43]: 'IV | CAPE HATTERAS | *The seas all crossed,* | *weathered the capes, the voyage done* . . . | –WALT WHITMAN'. p. [44]: blank. pp. 45–53: text of "Cape Hatteras." p. [54]: blank. p. [55]: 'V | THREE SONGS | *The one Sestos, the other Abydos hight.* | –MARLOWE'. p. [56]: blank. pp. 57–62: text of "Three Songs." p. [63]: 'VI | QUAKER HILL | *I see only the ideal. But no ideals* | *have ever been fully successful on* | *this earth.* |

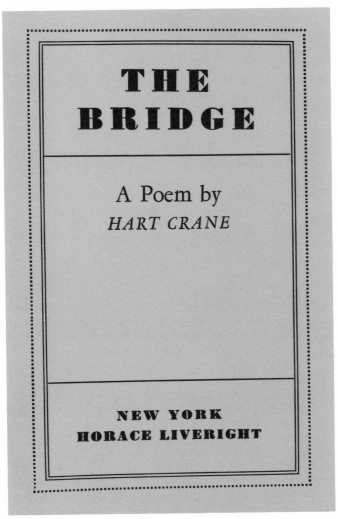

THE BRIDGE

A Poem by
HART CRANE

**NEW YORK
HORACE LIVERIGHT**

Title page of the second edition of *The Bridge*, first impression
(A 3.1)

—ISADORA DUNCAN | *The gentian weaves her fringes,* | *The maple's loom is red.* | —EMILY DICKINSON'. p. [64]: blank. pp. 65–67: text of "Quaker Hill." p. [68]: blank. p. [69]: 'VII | THE TUNNEL | *To Find the Western path* | *Right thro'* *the Gates of Wrath.* | —BLAKE'. p. [70]: blank. pp. 71–76: text of "The Tunnel." p. [77]: 'VIII | ATLANTIS | *Music is then the* *knowledge of that which* | *relates to love in harmony and sys-* *tem.* | —PLATO'. p. [78]: blank. pp. 79–82: text of "Atlantis." pp. [83–84]: blank.

Illustration: A single leaf of coated, white, wove, unwater-marked paper inserted by gluing between p. [iv] and p. [1]. Recto: blank. Verso: in the upper third, a black and white half-tone photograph (2 5/16 × 4) of Brooklyn Bridge as seen from below and from one side in a perspective which shows a portion of one of the main pillars and the underside of the roadway; at bottom, '*Photograph by Walker Evans*'.

Typography: 32 ll., 6 17/32 (7) × 4 7/8. Text in 11-pt. Gara-mond; marginal notes in 10-pt. Garamond italic; poem titles in 14-pt. Ultra Bodoni; initial letters of poems in 30-pt. Ultra Bodoni. Running titles (e.g., 'THE BRIDGE' on verso, 'CAPE HATTERAS' on recto) in 8-pt. Ultra Bodoni; page numbers in 8-pt. Ultra Bodoni centered at foot of page.

Paper: White, laid (1 3/16 spaced chain lines, running verti-cally), watermarked with the word 'Utopian' beneath a flask-like figure enclosing a pair of scales suspended from a line that passes out of the neck of the figure, is interrupted by a small circle, and terminates at an 'X'. Leaves bulk 5/16; leaf thick-ness .0061.

Binding: Fine bead cloth (BF), dark blue. Front cover: within a blind-stamped single-rule frame (8 1/4 × 5 5/16), near the upper left-hand corner, 'THE BRIDGE' stamped in gilt. Spine: all stamped in gilt, reading vertically from the top, 'THE BRIDGE', followed by 'HART | CRANE', and at bottom, reading horizon-tally, an oval device containing the initials 'HL' and a silhouette of a monk at a lectern. Back: plain. White, wove, unwatermarked endpapers. Top cut; fore-edge and tail trimmed.

Dust jacket: Front cover: blue background, lettered in black, 'THE | BRIDGE | [black and white photograph (2 3/4 × 4 3/4) of Brooklyn Bridge as seen from below and from one side in a perspective which shows a portion of one of the main pillars and the underside of the roadway] | *by* HART CRANE | *author of* | "WHITE BUILDINGS" '. Spine: blue background, lettered in black, reading vertically from the top, 'THE BRIDGE *HART CRANE* [oval device containing the initials "HL" and the silhouette of a monk at a lectern] HORACE | LIVERIGHT'. Back cover: white background decorated top and bottom by three horizontal blue stripes, and between, all lettered in black, an advertisement of a second printing of *White Buildings* and quotations of comments on Crane's poetry by Eugene O'Neill, Waldo Frank, Edmund Wilson, and the London *Times Literary Supplement*. Front flap: white background, lettered in black, '$2.50 | THE BRIDGE | *by* HART CRANE | Author of *White Buildings*' followed by the text of a comment on Crane's poetry and, at bottom, a blue line and the notation '*Photograph on Jacket by* | WALKER EVANS'. Back flap: white background, lettered in black, with quotations of comments on Crane's poetry by Alfred Kreymborg, Yvor Winters, and *Vanity Fair*.

Notes: Publication. The first impression of the Liveright edition of *The Bridge* was printed from relief plates made from type set by Van Rees Book Composition Company of 518 Twenty-sixth Street, New York, N.Y.; printing was completed on March 12, 1930. The original plates were used again in the second printing of July 1930. According to a statement of operations dated December 31, 1930, 712 copies of *The Bridge* had been sold that year.[1] The copyright application for *The Bridge* gives March 22, 1930, as the date of publication, and shows the printer to have been Van Rees Press (same address as above) and the binding to have been performed by Van Rees Bindery, 304 Hudson St., New York, N.Y. In *Publishers' Weekly* for March 8, 1930, *The Bridge* was advertised as available in April. The accession date of the Library of Congress copyright deposit was March 26, 1930.

Text. In preparing the text of *The Bridge* for the New York edition, Crane made many corrections and alterations, with the result that the text of the New York edition differed from the Paris edition published three months earlier. We know from Crane's correspondence that he composed the "Cape Hatteras" section of the poem hurriedly in order to meet the schedule of the Paris printer. Hence, he made the most changes in this section for the New York edition. The changes between the two editions involved minor alterations in spelling, punctuation, and typography as well as more significant additions, deletions,

---

1. See Walker Gilmer, *Horace Liveright: Publisher of the Twenties* (New York: David Lewis, 1970), p. 257.

and changes in words, phrases, and entire lines. The following examples are characteristic:

Paris: But the eagle that dominates our days, is jurist (p. 6o)
New York: Now the eagle dominates our days, is jurist (p. 46)

Paris: Of you – the theme that's statured in the cliff, (p. 61)
New York: Of you – the theme that's statured in the cliff. (p. 47)

Paris: Glow from the great stones of the prison crypt
         That is each canyoned street. Your eyes, confronting the Exchange
         Surviving in a world of stocks, also keep range (p. 61)
New York: Gleam from the great stones of each prison crypt
         Of canyoned traffic . . . Confronting the Exchange,
         Surviving in a world of stocks, – they also range (p. 47)

Paris: Of dynamos where (p. 61)
New York: Of dynamos, where (p. 47)

Paris: By naptha fledged (p. 62)
New York: By naphtha fledged (p. 48)

Paris: The blue's unfeathered districts unto aether . . . (p. 62)
New York: The blue's cloud templed districts unto ether . . . (p. 48)

Paris: Hell's belt springs wider – into heaven's plumed side. (p. 62)
New York: Hell's belt springs wider into heaven's plumed side. (p. 48)

Paris: The wounds we wrap with theorems sharp as hail! (p. 63)
New York: Wounds that we wrap with theorems sharp as hail! (p. 48)

Paris: New scouting griffons rise through gaseous crepe (p. 64)
New York: See scouting griffons rise through gaseous crepe (p. 49)

Paris: To conjugate infinity's dim marge (p. 64)
New York: To conjugate infinity's dim marge – (p. 49)

Paris: Lift agonized quittance, tilt from the invisible brink
            (p. 64)
New York: Lift agonized quittance, tilting from the invisible
               brink (p. 50)

Paris: Down
                whizzing (p. 65)
New York: Down whizzing (p. 50)

Paris: Vortex into
                    crashed (p. 65)
New York: Vortex into crashed (p. 50)

Paris: Ghoul mound of man's inventiveness at baulk (p. 66)
New York: Ghoul-mound of man's perversity at balk (p. 51)

Paris: Potomac lilies, then the Pontiac rose (p. 66)
New York: Potomac lilies, – then the Pontiac rose, (p. 51)

Paris: As vibrantly, (p. 67)
New York: As vibrantly (p. 51)

Paris: Familiar, thou, as mendicants in public places, (p. 67)
New York: Familiar, thou, as mendicants in public places;
               (p. 52)

Paris: Evasive–too–as daysprings spreading arc to trace is,
            – (p. 67)
New York: Evasive–too–as daysprings spreading arc to
               trace is; – (p. 52)

Paris: Recorders ages hence, ah, they shall hear (p. 68)
New York: Recorders ages hence, yes, they shall hear (p. 53)

A 3.2

Second impression: A second impression was made in July
1930; the number of copies is undetermined. It differed from
the first impression in the following ways:

Collation: Same as for the first impression except that there
was no cancel at 6_1. The plate used to print the cancellans for
the first impression was used again to impose the recto of the
conjugate 6_1 of the second impression.

Contents: P. [2] was modified to read, 'COPYRIGHT, 1930,
BY HORACE LIVERIGHT, INC. | MANUFACTURED IN THE
U.S.A. | First printing, April, 1930 | Second printing, July,
1930'.

Illustrations: In place of the photograph used for the first impression there was substituted a black and white halftone photograph (5 27/32 × 4) of Brooklyn Bridge in a perspective which shows a main pillar as seen through the suspension cables.

Paper: White, laid (1 5/8 spaced chain lines, running vertically), watermarked with an oval device enclosing the initials 'HL' and the outline of a monk at a lectern. Leaves bulk 1/4.

A 3.3
Third impression: A third impression was made in October 1970 from lithographic plates, with introductory material added and pagination altered. The title page and text of the poem were printed from plates derived by photographic process from a copy of the first impression of March 1930, with the publisher's imprint and pagination altered. New introductory matter was added: an introduction dated 1970 by Thomas A. Vogler and the introduction by Waldo Frank that was first printed in *The Collected Poems of Hart Crane,* 1933. This new matter was printed from plates made by photographic process from proof sheets printed from type set by York Typesetting, 480 Canal Street, New York, N.Y. Sheets for 5,000 copies were printed by the Halliday Lithograph Corp., Circuit Street, West Hanover, Mass. The paperback cover was printed by Rapoport Printing Corp. of 195 Hudson Street, New York, N.Y. Binding was done by Halliday Lithograph Corp. at their Plimpton, Mass., bindery in an initial order of 2,500 copies; as of January 1, 1971, sheets for the remaining 2,500 copies were stored at the bindery. This impression differed from the first and second in the following ways:

Title page: As for the 1930 impressions, except that the text is entirely in black and the publisher's imprint at the bottom was changed to the following: '[silhouette of a monk at a lectern] | LIVERIGHT | NEW YORK'.

Collation: (8 3/16 × 5 3/16): 56 leaves, pp. [i-viii] ix-xv [xvi] xvii-xxxvi 1-2 [3-4] 5-8 [9-10] 11-29 [30-32] 33-36 [37-38] 39-47 [48-50] 51-56 [57-58] 59-61 [62-64] 65-70 [71-72] 73-76.

Contents: p. [i]: 'THE BRIDGE'. p. [ii]: blank. p. [iii]: title page. p. [iv]: 'Copyright © 1933, 1958, 1970 by | LIVERIGHT PUBLISHING CORPORATION. | All rights reserved. No part of this book may be reproduced in any | form without permission in writing from the publisher. | 1.987654321 | SBN 87140-040-5 | Library of Congress Card Number 79-131276 | LIVERIGHT

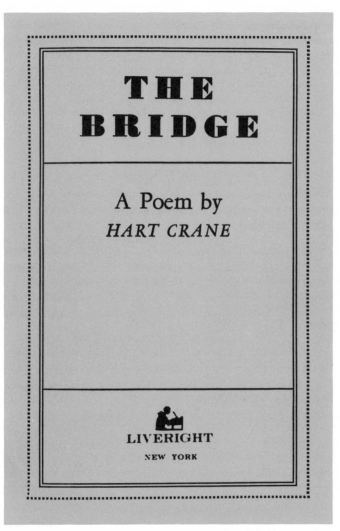

THE BRIDGE

A Poem by
HART CRANE

LIVERIGHT
NEW YORK

Title page of the second edition of *The Bridge*, third impression
(A 3.3)

PAPERBOUND EDITION 1970 | MANUFACTURED IN THE
UNITED STATES OF AMERICA'. p. [v]: '*From going to and
fro in the earth,* | *and from walking up and down in it.* | THE
BOOK OF JOB'. p. [vi]: blank, pp. [vii–viii]: table of contents.
pp. ix–xv: introduction by Thomas A. Vogler. p. [xvi]: blank.
pp. xvii–xxxvi: introduction by Waldo Frank. pp. 1–76: text of
The Bridge, corresponding to pp. 7–82 of the 1930 impressions.

Illustrations: No illustrations were included with this impression.

Paper: White, wove, unwatermarked. Leaves bulk 3/4.

Binding: Paperback. Front, spine, and back have a lavender
background which deepens to purple at the bottom of the front,
spine, and lower back cover. Front cover: in the upper right,
'Liveright L-25 $1.95'; beneath, at left, '[in purple] Hart Crane's
| The | Bridge | Commentaries by | Waldo Frank and Thomas A.
Vogler'; the bottom two-thirds of the front cover contains a
stylized representation of Brooklyn Bridge as seen from beneath,
with the roadway and cables represented in black and the supporting pillars in orange at the top shading into lavender at the
bottom. Spine: reading vertically from top to bottom, '[in purple]
Hart Crane's [in black] The Bridge'; reading horizontally, at
bottom, '[silhouette of a monk at a lectern] | LIVERIGHT |
[in white] L-25'. Back cover: at upper left, 'Poetry | [in purple]
Hart Crane's | The | Bridge'; followed by quotations from critical
comments by Malcolm Cowley, Eugene O'Neill, Henri Peyre,
and the New York Herald-Tribune; and, at bottom left, '[in pur-
ple] COVER DESIGN BY AL NAGY | Liveright | 386 Park Ave-
nue South | New York, N.Y. 10016'. The verso of the front cover
and recto of the back cover are white and blank; the exterior
cover surfaces are coated with a transparent plastic laminate.

Notes to section A 3:   Library of Congress copyright deposit.
PS3505.R272B7 1930 (first impression).

> *Copies examined.*
> HM: ALA 1516.20.5 (second impression, rebound)
> ICN: Y/285/.C8555 (first impression)
> ICN: Case/4a/413 (first impression; M. D. Zabel's copy dated
>   April 1930)
> ICU: PS/3506/.R21B8/1930/MoPo (first impression)
> ICU: PS/3506/.R21B8/1930/copy 2/MoPo (second impres-
>   sion, rebound)
> ICU: PS/3506/.R21/B8/1930/Cop. 3 (first impression)
> IEN: Rare Book Room/Am/C89lbr/1930 (first impression)

Liveright Publishing Corporation library (third impression)
NBu: Rare Book Room (first impression, lacks free endpaper
        at back)
NBuU: Poetry Room (first impression with dust jacket)
NNC: Carpenter/D812C852/05 (first impression, rebound)
NNC: Special Collections/B812 C849/05/1930a (second impression)
NNC: Special Collections/B812C849/05/1930a (second imsion)
OCl: 811.5/C8497b (first impression rebound)
OU: EL 140/C8905/Br. (second impression, rebound)
WMM: Rare Book Room/CVK2 (first impression)
University of London Library: U.S./811.5/CRA (first impression)
Compilers' personal copies of third impression

A 4 THE COLLECTED POEMS OF HART CRANE
First edition

A 4.1
First impression

Title page: THE COLLECTED POEMS | OF | [in red] HART
CRANE | [rule (3 27/32)] | EDITED WITH | AN INTRODUC-
TION BY | WALDO FRANK | [two vine and leaf devices, in red,
arranged with curled stem ends toward one another and, pointing outward along each stem, the same arrangement of five
leaves] | [rule (3 27/32)] | LIVERIGHT · INC · PUBLISHERS |
NEW YORK

Collation: (8 5/8 × 6 1/4): [unsigned, 1–13⁸ 14⁴], 108 leaves,
pp. [i–vi] vii–xxix [xxx] xxxi–xxxiv [1–2] 3–58 [59–60]`61–110
[111–112] 113–139 [140–142] 143–159 [160–162] 163–172
[173–174] 175–179 [180–182].

Contents: p. [i]: 'THE COLLECTED POEMS OF | HART
CRANE'. p. [ii]: blank. p. [iii]: title page. p. [iv]: 'COPYRIGHT,
1933, LIVERIGHT, INC. | MANUFACTURED IN THE UNITED
STATES OF AMERICA | AT THE VAN REES PRESS'. p. [v]:
headed 'EDITOR'S NOTE | [rule (3 27/32)]' and followed by
the text of the note. p. [vi]: blank. pp. vii–xxix: introduction by
Waldo Frank, dated New York, December 1932 and arranged in
four parts with divisions marked by lowercase italic letters.
p. [xxx]: blank. pp. xxxi–xxxiv: table of contents. p. [1]: 'ONE
THE BRIDGE | [rule (3 13/16)] | *From going to and fro in the
earth,* | *and from walking up and down in it.* | THE BOOK OF
JOB'. p. [2]: blank. pp. 3–58: text. p. [59]: 'TWO · WHITE
BUILDINGS | [rule (3 13/16)] | *Ce ne peut être que la fin du
monde, en* | *avançant.* –RIMBAUD'. p. [60]: 'TO WALDO
FRANK'. pp. 61–110: text. p. [111]: 'THREE · KEY WEST |
AN ISLAND SHEAF | [rule (3 27/32)] | *The starry floor,* | *The
wat'ry shore,* | *Is given thee 'til the break of day.* | –BLAKE'.
p. [112]: blank. pp. 113–139: text. p. [140]: blank. p. [141]:
'FOUR · UNCOLLECTED POEMS | [rule (3 27/32)]'. p. [142]:
blank. pp. 143–159: text. p. [160]: blank. p. [161]: 'APPENDIX
A. | EARLY POEMS | [rule (3 13/16)]'. p. [162]: editor's note.
pp. 163–172: text. p. [173]: 'APPENDIX B. | MODERN PO-
ETRY: AN ESSAY | [rule (3 13/16)]'. p. [174]: blank. pp. 175–
179: text. pp. [180–182]: blank.

Items included: Editor's note; Introduction by Waldo Frank;
THE BRIDGE; Proem: To Brooklyn Bridge; Ave Maria; Pow-

THE COLLECTED POEMS

OF

HART CRANE

EDITED WITH

AN INTRODUCTION BY

WALDO FRANK

LIVERIGHT·INC·PUBLISHERS

NEW YORK

Title page of the first edition of *The Collected Poems of Hart Crane*, first impression (A 4.1)

hatan's Daughter; The Harbour Dawn; Van Winkle; The River; The Dance; Indiana; Cutty Sark; Cape Hatteras; Three Songs; Southern Cross; National Winter Garden; Virginia; Quaker Hill; The Tunnel; Atlantis; WHITE BUILDINGS; Legend; Black Tambourine; Emblems of Conduct; My Grandmother's Love Letters; Sunday Morning Apples; Praise for an Urn; Garden Abstract; Stark Major; Chaplinesque; Pastorale; In Shadow; The Fernery; North Labrador; Repose of Rivers; Paraphrase; Possessions; Lachrymae Christi; Passage; The Wine Menagerie; Recitative; For the Marriage of Faustus and Helen; At Melville's Tomb; Voyages I, II, III, IV, VI; KEY WEST: AN ISLAND SHEAF; Key West; O Carib Isle!; The Mango Tree; Island Quarry; The Merman; The Idiot; A Name for All; Royal Palm; The Air Plant; Imperator Victus; The Hurricane; Bacardi Spreads the Eagle's Wings; And Bees of Paradise; To Emily Dickinson; Moment Fugue; To the Cloud Juggler; By Nilus Once I Knew . . . ; To Shakespeare; The Broken Tower; The Phantom Bark; March; Old Song; UNCOLLECTED POEMS; A Traveler Born; Enrich My Resignation; The Sad Indian; The Circumstance; The Visible the Untrue; Reliquary; Purgatorio; Havana Rose; Reply; A Postscript; Eternity; The Return; EARLY POEMS; The Hive; Annunciation; The Bathers; Modern Craft; Carrier Letter; October-November; Fear; Postscript; To Potapovitch; Forgetfulness; Modern Poetry: An Essay.

The following poems are included in this edition, as well as in the 1938 edition, and in *The Complete Poems,* 1958, but do not appear in *The Complete Poems,* 1966: "A Traveler Born," "Enrich My Resignation," "The Circumstance," and "The Return."

Illustration: A single leaf of coated, white, wove, unwatermarked paper tipped in between pp. [ii] and [iii]. Recto, blank; verso contains a black and white photograph (5 3/16 × 3 11/16) of a portrait of Hart Crane surrounded by a white border (1/8) within a red rule frame (1/16 thick, external dimensions 5 9/16 × 4 1/16) and, at bottom, the caption, 'HART CRANE | *From a portrait by David Alfaro Siqueiros'.*

Typography: 28 ll. (introduction) and 30 ll. (text of poems), 5 15/16 (6 7/16) × 4 9/16. Introduction in 12-pt. Bodoni Book; text of poems in 12-pt. Bodoni Book; initial letters of poems in 20-pt.; poem titles in 14-pt.; running titles in 8-pt.; page numbers in 12-pt., centered at the foot of the page.

Paper: White, laid (chain lines spaced 13/16, running vertically), watermarked with the outline of a book having the initial 'R' on the cover, streamers on either side, and, above, the words 'Louvain Book'. Leaves bulk 5/8; leaf thickness .0057.

Binding: Sand patterned cloth (C), dark maroon. Front cover: within a blind-stamped rule compartment (8 3/16 × 5 5/16), 'THE | COLLECTED POEMS | OF HART CRANE' stamped in gilt. Spine: reading horizontally, all stamped in gilt, 'THE | COLLECTED | POEMS | OF | HART | CRANE' and, at bottom, 'LIVERIGHT'. Back cover: plain. White, wove, unwatermarked endpapers. Top cut; tail and fore-edge trimmed.

Dust jacket: Front cover: brown background lettered in white, '*THE* | COLLECTED | POEMS | *of* | HART | CRANE'. Spine: brown background lettered in black, reading horizontally, 'The | Collected | Poems | of | HART | CRANE | Edited | with | an | Introduction | by | WALDO | FRANK' and, at bottom, 'Liveright | Inc.'. Back cover: white background with a sepia-tone photograph (4 7/8 × 4 1/2) and, beneath, the identification, 'HART CRANE'; at bottom, on the left, three vertical rules (each 1 1/8) and the text, "In the judgment of many leading critics of America and Europe, Hart Crane is the most important of our poets since Walt Whitman." Front flap: white background with price marked as $2.50 and, beneath, a descriptive comment concluding, "This volume, therefore, represents a definitive edition of the poems of Hart Crane." Rear flap: excerpts of comments by Eugene O'Neill, Yvor Winters, the *New York Evening Post,* Malcolm Cowley, and the London *Times.*

Presentation copies
Fifty presentation copies were prepared, identical with other copies of the first impression except for these differences:

Contents: On p. [ii] presentation copies have the note: 'FIFTY COPIES OF THIS WORK | HAVE BEEN SET ASIDE | FOR PRESENTATION ONLY TO THE | FRIENDS OF HART CRANE | *This copy is numbered* | [four parallel rules (each 11/16) arranged for the number to be stamped over them]'.

Binding: Brown cloth. On the front cover the rule compartment is stamped in black, but in all other respects the front cover, spine, and back are treated exactly as for the trade-copy binding. Endpapers: the visible side of the lining papers and the corresponding sides of the free endpapers are black; the other sides of the free endpapers are white.

Notes: Copies were numbered by stamping in blue ink. The copy in the library of Ohio State University was originally stamped "55" and the second five is still visible although at some time an effort was made to erase it and to substitute in pencil an "0".

Notes to section A 4.1: *Publication. Collected Poems* was published on March 24, 1933. This impression was from relief plates made from type set by Van Rees Book Composition Company of 518 Twenty-sixth Street, New York, N.Y.; the first printing was completed on March 13, 1933. The copyright application for *The Collected Poems of Hart Crane* gives March 24, 1933, as the date of publication and shows the printer to have been Van Rees Press (same address as above) and the binding to have been performed by Montauk Book Binding Corporation, New York, N.Y. The book was advertised by Liveright in *Publishers' Weekly* of January 28, 1933, as available in February. The Library of Congress copyright deposit shows an accession date of November 25. We have been informed by Mr. Pell of the Liveright Publishing Corporation that he has no record of the number of copies printed in any of the Liveright impressions of *The Collected Poems of Hart Crane;* unfortunately, the relevant records of the Van Rees Press for this period were ruined by water so that no information has been available from this source either.

The choice of Waldo Frank as editor was the subject of some controversy. In an article in *The New English Weekly* (June 23, 1932), Gorham Munson asserted that he had seen a printed announcement that E. E. Cummings was to be the editor of *The Collected Poems;* we have been unable to discover any such announcement. Waldo Frank, in his rejoinder in *The New English Weekly* (July 21, 1932), made clear that Mrs. Crane had selected him as the editor of the volume. Frank's statement appears to be supported by the recollection of Samuel Loveman (*Hart Crane: A Conversation With Samuel Loveman,* edited by Jay Socin and Kirby Congdon [New York: Interim Books, 1964]) who many years later testified that Frank had been chosen instead of him because at the time Frank had a more prominent reputation in literary circles.

First state of the first impression. In Merle Johnson's *American First Editions,* 3rd ed. (rev. Jacob Blanck [New York: R. R. Bowker, 1936]), p. 122, there is an assertion that a first state of the first impression of *The Collected Poems* lacks the "period" after 'INC' on the title page. All copies that we have examined – including the uncorrected proof copy sent by Liveright to Morton D. Zabel – have the form 'LIVERIGHT · INC · PUBLISHERS'. It seems likely, then, that if copies do exist lacking the dot after 'INC', these would probably constitute a later rather than an earlier state, resulting from damage to the plate in the course of the first impression.

Text. The text of *The Collected Poems* which Waldo Frank prepared for publication included a section entitled "Key West: An Island Sheaf." Crane apparently contemplated a collection of his poems to be so titled, and he had progressed so far as to have prepared a title page with an epigram by Blake. The folder containing these poems, now at Columbia University library, includes a table of contents listing thirteen poems: "O Carib Isle!," "The Mermen," "To the Cloud Juggler," "The Mango Tree," "Island Quarry," "Old Song," "The Idiot," "A Name for All," "Connecticut-Cubano Overheard" ("Bacardi Spreads the Eagle's Wings"), "Imperator Victus," "Royal Palm," "The Air Plant," and "The Hour!" ("The Hurricane"). In addition, the folder contains drafts of seven other poems: "The Tree: Great William," "To Shakespeare," "Key West," "The Hurricane," "By Nilus Once I Knew . . . ," "Moment Fugue," and "To Emily Dickinson." It is not clear that Crane placed these drafts in the folder. Furthermore, the poems in the folder are not in the typed form which Crane ordinarily gave to his completed work. The appearance of these poems in the 1933 edition of *The Collected Poems* under the heading "Key West: An Island Sheaf" suggested a state of completeness which in fact these poems do not seem to have reached; subsequently, Brom Weber in his edition of *The Complete Poems and Selected Letters and Prose of Hart Crane* has made clear their status by including them with the uncollected Crane material.

A 4.2
Second impression: Identical with the first impression except for the following:

Title page: Printed from the plate used for the first impression, but with the line 'LIVERIGHT · INC · PUBLISHERS' deleted and replaced by the line 'LIVERIGHT PUBLISHING CORPORATION'.

Contents: The copyright notice on p. [iv] was altered to read, 'COPYRIGHT, 1933, LIVERIGHT, INC. | LIVERIGHT PUBLISHING CORPORATION | MANUFACTURED IN | THE UNITED STATES OF AMERICA | AT THE VAN REES PRESS'.

Paper: Copies were printed both on a white, wove, unwatermarked paper (leaves bulk 11/16) and on a white, laid, unwatermarked paper (chain lines spaced 31/32, running vertically; leaves bulk 3/4).

Dust jacket: Front cover: brown background lettered in white, 'The | COLLECTED | POEMS | of | HART | CRANE'. Spine, from

THE COLLECTED POEMS
OF
HART CRANE

EDITED WITH

AN INTRODUCTION BY

WALDO FRANK

LIVERIGHT PUBLISHING CORPORATION

NEW YORK

Title page of the first edition of *The Collected Poems of Hart Crane,* second impression (A 4.2)

the top, all reading horizontally, all lettered in brown: on a white band (1 15/16), 'The | Collected | Poems | of | HART | CRANE'; a brown band (9/16); on a white band (1 9/16), 'Edited | with | an | Introduction | by | Waldo | Frank'; a brown band (3 1/2); on a white band (13/16), 'Liveright'. Back cover: advertisement of books in the Black & Gold Library series, all lettered in brown. Front and rear flaps: text as for the first impression dust jacket, but lettered in brown.

A 4.3
Third impression: Identical with the second impression except for the following:

Collation: [unsigned, 1–12^8 13^4 14^8].

Contents: The copyright notice on p. [iv] was altered by deleting the line 'AT THE VAN REES PRESS'.

Binding: Light orange cloth. Rule compartment blind-stamped on front cover measures 8 × 5.

A 4.4
Black & Gold edition: In 1946 a subsidiary edition of *The Collected Poems of Hart Crane* was printed from the 1933-edition plates and published in the Liveright Black & Gold Library series. Copies prepared for publication in this format differed from those of the third impression of the 1933 edition in the following ways:

Collation: As for the third impression, but with somewhat reduced leaf size (8 1/2 × 5 5/8) and a variation in the location of the 4-leaf gathering: [unsigned, 1–11^8 12^4 13–14^8].

Contents: On p. [iv] the copyright notice was adjusted to read, 'THE COLLECTED POEMS OF | HART CRANE | [star] | COPYRIGHT, 1933, LIVERIGHT INC. | LIVERIGHT PUBLISHING CORPORATION | [star] | *Copyright in All Countries* | [star] | BLACK & GOLD EDITION | JULY, 1946 | [star] | *Manufactured* | *in the United States of America*'.

Illustrations: A second illustration on a single leaf of coated, white, wove, unwatermarked paper was tipped in between pp. 58 and [59]. Recto, a black and white photograph of Hart Crane (7 × 4 1/4) and, beneath, the caption, 'HART CRANE | *From a photograph by Walker Evans*'; verso, blank.

Paper: White, laid (chain lines spaced 31/32, running vertically), unwatermarked. Leaves bulk 5/8; leaf thickness .0047.

THE COLLECTED POEMS
OF
HART CRANE

EDITED WITH

AN INTRODUCTION BY

WALDO FRANK

LIVERIGHT PUBLISHING CORPORATION

NEW YORK

Title page of the Black & Gold edition of *The Collected Poems of Hart Crane* (A 4.4)

Binding: Diagonal fine rib-cloth (S), black with lettering, rules, and fleurons all stamped in gilt; top and tail cut, fore-edge trimmed; top stained maroon. In general, the binding is consistent with other volumes in the Black & Gold Library series. Front cover: 'THE | COLLECTED POEMS | OF HART CRANE' and, at bottom, a reproduction of the signature of Hart Crane. Spine, from the top: a band of arabesque fleurons (1/2) bordered by a double rule above and a single rule below; a blue band (1 1/2) bordered at top and bottom by thick rules (1/16) and stamped, reading horizontally, 'THE | COLLECTED | POEMS | OF | HART CRANE'; single rules spaced 5 1/4 apart and enclosing ten bands of arabesque fleurons (each 1/2); a blue band (5/16) bordered at top and bottom by thick rules (1/16) and stamped 'LIVERIGHT'; a band of arabesque fleurons (1/2) bordered by a single rule above and a double rule below. Back cover: plain. Copies have been seen with two kinds of endpapers: (1) white, wove, unwatermarked and (2) with the visible side of the lining papers and corresponding side of the free endpapers coated black, and the other side of the free endpapers white.

Dust jacket: Front cover: on a yellow background, a photograph in red tones of a portrait of Hart Crane, surrounded by a red border (4 7/16 × 3 3/16), and beneath, '[in red] THE | [in green] Collected Poems of | [in red] HART CRANE'. Spine: reading horizontally from top, lettered in green, 'THE | Collected | Poems | of | [photograph in red tones of a portrait of Hart Crane, surrounded by a red border (1 5/16 × 1)] | HART | CRANE' and, at bottom, in red, 'LIVERIGHT'. Back cover: white background, containing advertisements of the Liveright Black & Gold Library. Front flap: title, author, indication of Waldo Frank's responsibility for editing and for the introduction, a descriptive comment on the contents, and an identification of the jacket illustration as from a portrait by David Alfaro Siqueiros. Back flap: quotations of critical notices by the *New York Herald Tribune,* Eugene O'Neill, *Poetry Magazine,* the *New York Evening Post,* Malcolm Cowley, and the *London Times.*

A 4.5
Second impression of Black & Gold edition: The order of the first two impressions is uncertain; it is clear, however, that there were two impressions, the second of which differs from that described above in the following ways:

Collation: (8 1/2 × 5 5/8): [unsigned, 1–12⁸ 13⁴ 14⁸].

A 5 TWO LETTERS

Title page: TWO LETTERS: | HART CRANE | To FREDER-
ICK CLAYTON | "Amicitiae Longaevitate" | BROOKLYN
HEIGHTS · NOVEMBER 1934

Collation: (8 7/16 × 5 7/16): [unsigned, 1²], 2 leaves, pp. [1–4].

Contents: p. [1]: title page. p. [2]: headed '*These letters are
printed through the kindness of | Grace Hart Crane and
Samuel Loveman.*' followed by a letter with salutation, 'Ahoy
Sam.', and closure, 'Love, | Hart.', dated 'R.M.S. "Tuscania" |
Off Newfoundland, | December 9, 1928.'. p. [3]: headed '*This
letter was written two weeks before Hart leaped into the sea.*'
followed by a letter with the salutation, 'Dear Sam –', and clo-
sure, 'Love, as always, | HART', dated '15 Calle Michoacan, |
Mixcoac, DF | April 13, 1932', and, at bottom, the note, '*Fifty
Copies – For the Friends of Jack Birss*'. p. [4]: blank.

Typography: 6 13/16 × 4 1/8. Text of letter dated December 9,
1928, in 10-pt. Vogue lightface with 2-pt. leading; text of letter
dated April 13, 1932, set solid in 10-pt. Vogue lightface. Editorial
notations in 10-pt. italic. Title on title page in 18-pt. Vogue bold.

Paper: White, wove, unwatermarked. Leaf thickness .005.

Binding: Unbound folio single sheet. The New York Public
Library copy is folded as a folio and is otherwise unbound; the
British Museum copy has been library bound in a folder of card-
board boards joined by a reddish brown cloth hinge.

Notes: Text.   The text of the letter dated December 9, 1928,
provides an abridged version of letter no. 312 printed on p. 331
of *The Letters of Hart Crane*, edited by Brom Weber, 1952. The
text of the letter dated April 13, 1932, provides a version which
in part abridges and in part expands letter no. 400 printed on
pp. 408–409 of Weber's edition of the letters.

> *Notations made in the text.*
> 1. The British Museum copy is signed at the bottom of p. [3],
>   'Jack Birss' and has the date '11:19:34', all in blue ink. The
>   British Museum stamp is dated December 8, 1934.
> 2. The New York Public Library copy has on p. [1] the pencil
>   note '(Dedication)' adjoining the line 'To FREDERICK
>   CLAYTON'; on p. [3] there is an asterisk in pencil in the
>   text after 'R – A – !' and a pencil note at the bottom, '*false
>   initials.'; on p. [4] there is a pencil note as follows: 'This

TWO LETTERS:
HART CRANE

To FREDERICK CLAYTON
"Amicitiae Longaevitate"

BROOKLYN HEIGHTS ● **NOVEMBER 1934**

Title page of *Two Letters* (A 5)

was printed on Fulton Street | (Brooklyn) near the site of Andrew Rome's printshop where *Leaves of Grass* | was first set in type. Of the name of the job printer I have no recollection. | J. B. | Brooklyn Heights | Nov. 25, 1949'. The New York Public Library copy is signed at the bottom of p. [3], 'Jack Birss', in blue ink.

Copies examined.
British Museum: 010920. b. 38
NBuU: Poetry Room
NN: *KVB/(1934, Nov.)

A 6 THE COLLECTED POEMS OF HART CRANE
Second edition

Title page: The | Collected Poems of | HART CRANE | *Edited with Introduction* | *by Waldo Frank* | BORISWOOD: LONDON

Collation: (8 5/8 × 5 5/8): [A]⁸ B–K⁸ L⁴, 84 leaves, pp. [1–8] 9–20 [21–22] 23–77 [78–80] 81–122 [123–124] 125–149 [150–152] 153–167 [168]. $1 signed; page numbers centered in the direction line, signatures near the outer margin.

Contents: p. [1]: 'THE COLLECTED POEMS OF HART CRANE' and, at bottom, a rectangular frame (13/16 × 3/4) enclosing the figure of a mushroom, cap at right, stem extending downward to left, with the letter 'B' above the stem and the mark 'Ltd' below. p. [2]: blank. p. [3]: title page. p. [4]: 'Printed in Guernsey, C.I., British Isles | by the Star and Gazette Ltd., for | BORISWOOD LIMITED, 59 Frith Street, | Soho Square, London, W.1. | First published November 1938 | COPYRIGHT'. pp. [5–7]: table of contents. p. [8]: 'EDITOR'S NOTE' followed by text of note. pp. 9–20: introduction by Waldo Frank arranged in three parts, with divisions marked by Roman numerals. p. [21]: 'I | THE BRIDGE | *From going to and fro in the earth,* | *and from walking up and down in it.* | THE BOOK OF JOB'. p. [22]: blank: pp. 23–77: text. p. [78]: blank. p. [79]: 'II | WHITE BUILDINGS | *Ce ne peut être que la fin du monde, en* | *avançant.* | RIMBAUD'. p. [80]: 'To WALDO FRANK'. pp. 81–122: text. p. [123]: 'III | KEY WEST | AN ISLAND SHEAF | *The starry floor,* | *The Wat'ry shore,* | *Is given thee 'til break of day.* | BLAKE'. p. [124]: blank. pp. 125–149: text. p. [150]: blank. p. [151]: 'IV | UNCOLLECTED POEMS'. p. [152]: blank. pp. 153–167: text. p. [168]: blank.

Items included: Introduction by Waldo Frank; I THE BRIDGE; Proem: To Brooklyn Bridge; Ave Maria; Powhatan's Daughter; The Harbor Dawn; Van Winkle; The River; The Dance; Indiana; Cutty Sark; Cape Hatteras; Three Songs; Southern Cross; National Winter Garden; Virginia; Quaker Hill; The Tunnel; Atlantis; II WHITE BUILDINGS; Legend; Black Tambourine; Emblems of Conduct; My Grandmother's Love-Letters; Sunday; Sunday Morning Apples; Praise for an Urn; Garden Abstract; Stark Major; Chaplinesque; Pastorale; In Shadow; The Fernery; North Labrador; Repose of Rivers; Paraphrase; Possessions; Lachrymae Christi; Passage; The Wine Menagerie; Recitative; For the Marriage of Faustus and Helen, I, II, III;

The
Collected Poems of
HART CRANE

Edited with Introduction
by Waldo Frank

BORISWOOD : LONDON

Title page of the second edition of *The Collected Poems of Hart Crane* (A 6)

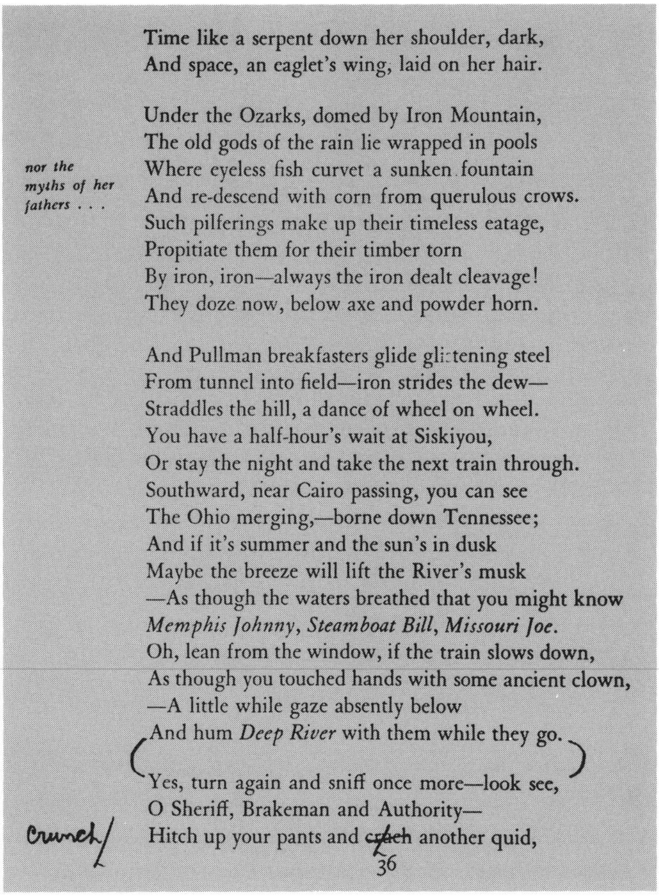

Time like a serpent down her shoulder, dark,
And space, an eaglet's wing, laid on her hair.

Under the Ozarks, domed by Iron Mountain,
The old gods of the rain lie wrapped in pools

nor the
myths of her
fathers . . .

Where eyeless fish curvet a sunken fountain
And re-descend with corn from querulous crows.
Such pilferings make up their timeless eatage,
Propitiate them for their timber torn
By iron, iron—always the iron dealt cleavage!
They doze now, below axe and powder horn.

And Pullman breakfasters glide glittening steel
From tunnel into field—iron strides the dew—
Straddles the hill, a dance of wheel on wheel.
You have a half-hour's wait at Siskiyou,
Or stay the night and take the next train through.
Southward, near Cairo passing, you can see
The Ohio merging,—borne down Tennessee;
And if it's summer and the sun's in dusk
Maybe the breeze will lift the River's musk
—As though the waters breathed that you might know
Memphis Johnny, Steamboat Bill, Missouri Joe.
Oh, lean from the window, if the train slows down,
As though you touched hands with some ancient clown,
—A little while gaze absently below
And hum *Deep River* with them while they go.

Yes, turn again and sniff once more—look see,
O Sheriff, Brakeman and Authority—
Hitch up your pants and ~~crack~~ another quid,

crunch

36

At Melville's Tomb; Voyages I, II, III, IV, V, VI; III KEY WEST: AN ISLAND SHEAF; Key West; O Carib Isle!; The Mango Tree; Island Quarry; The Merman; The Idiot; A Name for All; Royal Palm; The Air Plant; Imperator Victus; The Hurricane; Bacardi Spreads the Eagle's Wings; And Bees of Paradise; To Emily Dickinson; Moment Fugue; To the Cloud Juggler; By Nilus Once I Knew . . . ; To Shakespeare; The Tree; The Broken Tower; The Phantom Bark; March; Old Song; IV UNCOLLECTED POEMS; A Traveller Born; Enrich My Resignation; The Sad Indian; The Circumstance; The Visible the Untrue; Reliquary; Purgatorio; Havana Rose; Reply; A Postscript; Eternity; The Return.

The "Introduction" by Waldo Frank is an abridgment of the one that appeared in the 1933 edition of *Collected Poems*. The following items included in the 1933 edition of *Collected Poems* do not appear in the 1938 edition: "The Hive," "Annunciations," "The Bathers," "Modern Craft," "Carrier Letter," "October-November," "Fear," "Postscript," "To Potapovitch," "Forgetfulness," and "Modern Poetry: An Essay." This edition prints "The Tree" as a separate poem. The *Collected Poems, 1933*, and the *Complete Poems, 1958*, print it as a variant version of "To Shakespeare."

Typography: 31 ll., 5 7/8 (6 1/8) × 3 13/16. Text in 12-pt. Granjon with 2-pt. leading; table of contents and poem titles in 10-pt. Granjon; title on title page in 18-pt. Goudy Modern.

Paper: White, wove, unwatermarked. Leaves bulk 9/16; leaf thickness .0061.

Binding: Bound in rough gray cloth irregularly flecked with random threads of red, blue, brown, orange, green, and yellow, all running parallel, in some copies vertically, in others horizontally. Lettering in script type. Front cover: 'The | Collected Poems of | Hart Crane' stamped in red. Spine: reading vertically, 'The Collected Poems of Hart Crane' stamped in red. Back cover: plain. White, wove, unwatermarked endpapers. Top cut and stained maroon; tail and fore-edge trimmed.

Dust jacket: Tan paper. Front cover: in script type. '*The* COLLECTED POEMS of HART CRANE' and, at bottom in sans serif, 'BORISWOOD'. Spine: reading vertically, in script type, '*The Collected Poems of Hart Crane*' and, at bottom, arranged horizontally, a square enclosing the figure of a mushroom and the letters 'B' and 'Ltd'. Rear cover: advertisements of the poetry of Archibald Macleish. Front flap: at top, 'The first publication of the definitive | edition of the Poems of Hart Crane in this |

country is an event of importance.' followed by a paragraph on Crane's reputation and a paragraph of comment by Eugene O'Neill, in which O'Neill's name is misspelled as *O'Neil,* and concluding with a brief quotation from the *Times.* Back flap: blank.

Notes: Publication. The Boriswood Ltd. edition of *The Collected Poems of Hart Crane* was published in November 1938. Publication appears to have been delayed more than once. A corrected proof copy, now in the poetry room of the library of the State University of New York at Buffalo, has on p. [4] the printed wording, "First Published May 1938," with the word *May* crossed out and the word *September* added in pencil. The book was advertised in *The Bookseller* of October 6, 1938, as ready on November 11. The earliest accession date of a copyright deposit copy is that of the British Museum on November 12. We have been unable to locate any records of Boriswood Ltd., which was purchased by John Lane in 1938 and later taken over by Bodley Head publishers of Bow Street, London; and the records of the firm which printed the book, the *Star and Gazette* Ltd., were not retained when that firm was purchased by the *Guernsey Herald* in 1946. As a result, the number of copies printed is unknown, but the relative scarcity of copies in England would suggest that the initial printing was not large and that there were no subsequent impressions.

Copies examined.
British Museum: 11688.P.1
ICU: PS/3506/.R21/1938 (rebound)
NBuU: Poetry Room (one copy with dust jacket, and one
          copy of corrected page proof in tan paper wrapper)
Oxford University, Bodleian Library: 28121e.518
University Library, Cambridge: 721.c.93.61

A 7 THE LETTERS OF HART CRANE 1916–1932

A 7.1
First impression

Title page: THE LETTERS OF | HART CRANE | 1916–1932 |
EDITED BY BROM WEBER | *The imaged Word, it is, that holds
| Hushed willows anchored in its glow. | It is the unbetrayable
reply | Whose accent no farewell can know.* | HERMITAGE
HOUSE · NEW YORK

Collation: (8 5/16 × 5 9/16): [unsigned, 1–14¹⁶], 224 leaves,
pp. [i–iv] v–xiii [xiv] xv–xvi [xvii–xviii] [1–2] 3–110 [111–112]
113–227 [228–230] 231–360 [361–362] 363–413 [414] 415–426
[427–430].

Contents: p. [i]: 'THE LETTERS OF HART CRANE'. p. [ii]:
'*By Brom Weber* | HART CRANE: A BIOGRAPHICAL AND
CRITICAL STUDY, 1948'. p. [iii]: title page. p. [iv]: 'COPY-
RIGHT, 1952, BY BROM WEBER | *All rights reserved* | *First
Edition* | PRINTED IN THE UNITED STATES OF AMERICA'.
p. v: headed 'PREFACE' followed by text. pp. vi–xiii: text of
preface by Brom Weber. p. [xiv]: blank. p. xv: headed 'CHRO-
NOLOGY' followed by text. p. xvi: conclusion of text of chronology. p. [xvii]: headed 'CONTENTS' followed by table of con-
tents. p. [xviii]: blank. p. [1]: 'PART ONE | Ohio | (1916–1922)'.
p. [2]: blank. pp. 3–110: text. p. [111]: 'PART TWO | New York |
(1923–1925)'. p. [112]: blank. pp. 113–227: text. p. [228]: blank.
p. [229]: 'PART THREE | West Indies-Europe | (1926–1930)'.
p. [230]: blank. pp. 231–360: text. p. [361]: 'PART FOUR |
Mexico | (1931–1932)'. p. [362]: blank. pp. 363–412: text. p. 413:
headed 'LIST OF CORRESPONDENTS | (*Numbers are those of
the letters)*' followed by two-column list. p. [414]: blank. p. 415:
headed 'INDEX | (Asterisks denote works of Hart Crane)' fol-
lowed by two-column text of index. pp. 416–426: text of index.
pp. [427–430]: blank.

Illustration: A leaf of coated white paper tipped in between
pp. [ii] and [iii]. Recto: blank. Verso: a halftone photograph
(6 1/2 × 4 1/4) of Hart Crane, captioned at bottom, '*H. W. Minns* |
HART CRANE | (*Taken c.* 1921)'.

Typography: 42 ll., 6 1/2 (6 11/16) × 4 5/32. Text in 10-pt.
Baskerville Linotype cast on 11-pt. body; running titles – e.g.,
recto, 'OHIO (1916–1922)' and verso, 'THE LETTERS OF HART
CRANE' – and letter titles – e.g., '77: TO GORHAM MUNSON' –

THE LETTERS OF
HART CRANE

1916-1932

EDITED BY BROM WEBER

The imaged Word, it is, that holds
Hushed willows anchored in its glow.
It is the unbetrayable reply
Whose accent no farewell can know.

HERMITAGE HOUSE · NEW YORK

Title page of *The Letters of Hart Crane 1916–1932*, first impression (A 7.1)

281: To Allen Tate

Dear Allen: —/—/ As to the *briefer*,[1] I think that you give good rea-

1. Review of *White Buildings* in *The Dial* (Feb. 1927).

sons for assuming that Aiken wrote it. It might be more satisfying
to ascertain this more definitely—but I do not feel that beyond that
there is any particular justification for attacking him. He has a perfect right to claim that many of the poems are specious, and call
them intellectual fakes, etc. He may quite well believe that he is
right on the score. For years, remember, perfectly honest people
have seen nothing but insanity in such things as [Blake's] "The
Tiger"—The only pity is what can be done about it. You have
Aiken's sentimentality beautifully defined. Personally the man is
rather likeable, but I think he is full of poison. Let people like Hem-
ingway have every convert they want. When he writes something
vulnerable and signs it—we can backfire—and publicly—and that's
the only worthwhile way to spend—"we have so little breath to
lose." Thanks for the Davidson review. I certainly appreciate its
tone of honesty and sincerity. A copy of *transition* #1 has reached
me—and I'm enthusiastic about it. By all means send Jolas some
poems—and why not your article on Marianne Moore? It doesn't
spoil re-sale of ms. over here, you know. *transition* has some weak
contribs, of course, but the majority is respectable. Joyce, Gertrude
Stein, Williams, Winters, Laura [Riding], Larbaud, Gide, MacLeish,
Soùpault, etc. It's a wedge that ought to be used. Malcolm [Cowley]
also ought to send things—and it seems to have a proof-reader!

Aunt Harriet [Monroe] has taken "Cutty Sark"—of all things—
and I feel more cheerful. Have you sent her anything recently? Now
seems to be the time. —/—/

A portion of page 294 of *The Letters of Hart Crane 1916–1932*,
first impression, showing misplaced footnote in the text of letter
no. 281 (A 7.1)

in 11-pt. Baskerville Linotype. Title on title page in 30-pt. and 36-pt. Weiss Roman. Page numbering at the outer margin of the headline except for the first pages of text beginning major sections, where the number is centered at the foot of the page. On p. 121 the letter heading '132: To Gorham Munson' is upside down; on pp. 197 and 294 the footnotes were set in the text rather than at the bottom of the page.

Paper: White, wove, unwatermarked. Leaves bulk 1 1/4; leaf thickness .0053.

Binding: Irregular calico cloth (V), black. Front cover: plain. Spine: reading vertically, '*The Letters of* HART CRANE' and, at bottom, reading horizontally, 'HERMITAGE', all stamped in gilt. Back cover: plain. White, wove, unwatermarked endpapers. Top, fore-edge, and tail cut; top stained gold.

Dust jacket: Front cover: on a black background, '[in white fancy lettering] *The Letters of* | [in yellow] HART | [in yellow] CRANE | [in white] *1916–1932* | [photograph of Hart Crane] | [in yellow] *Edited by* BROM WEBER'. Spine: reading horizontally, '[in yellow fancy lettering] The | Letters | of'; reading vertically, top to bottom, '[in white] HART CRANE', and, at bottom, reading horizontally, '[in white] HERMITAGE'. Back cover: all white background with black lettering, quotations from Horace Gregory and Marya Zaturenska, and notes on Brom Weber, on Nettie Weber, and on Hervey Minns; price given as $5.00. Front and rear flaps: all on white background, headed '$5.00 | *The Letters of* | HART CRANE' and followed by descriptive comment on Crane's life and letters.

Notes: Publication. This impression was from plastic letter-press plates made from type set by the Stone Typesetting Company, Brattleboro, Vt. The original copyright application for *The Letters of Hart Crane 1916–1932* gives September 15, 1952, as the date of publication, and shows the printer and binder to have been American Book–Stratford Press of 75 Varick Street, New York, N.Y. The Library of Congress copyright deposit was accessioned on September 19, 1952. The number of copies is unknown.

A 7.2
Second impression: A second impression of 6,000 copies was made in 1965 from lithographic plates made by a photographic process from a corrected copy (see the "Copies examined" note which follows) of the first impression. The printer was Murray Printing Company, Forge Village, Mass., and the binder was

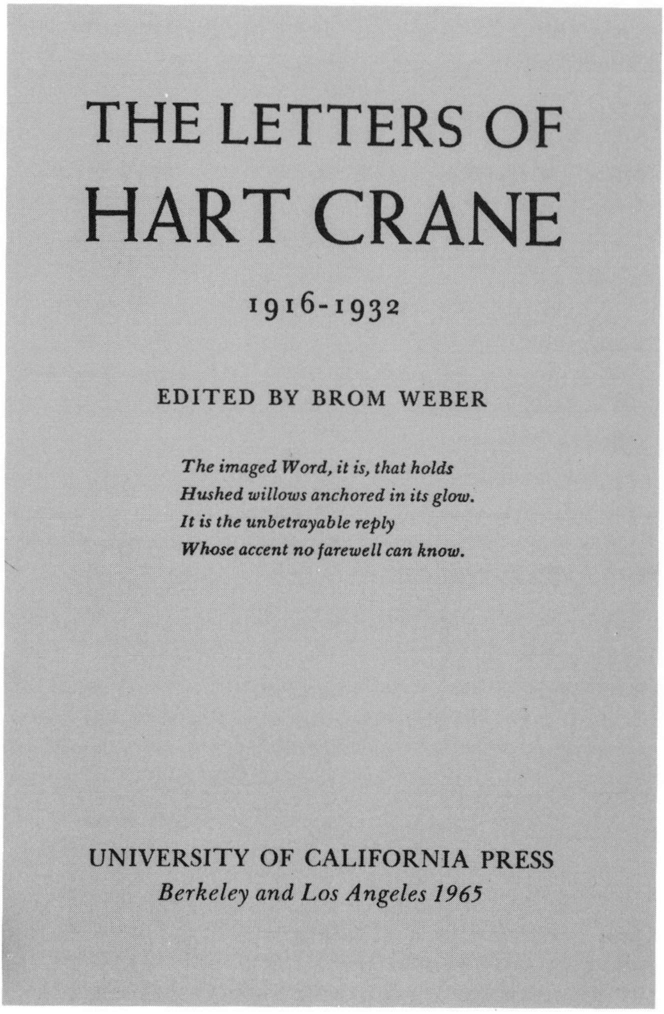

THE LETTERS OF

HART CRANE

1916-1932

EDITED BY BROM WEBER

The imaged Word, it is, that holds
Hushed willows anchored in its glow.
It is the unbetrayable reply
Whose accent no farewell can know.

UNIVERSITY OF CALIFORNIA PRESS
Berkeley and Los Angeles 1965

Title page of *The Letters of Hart Crane 1916–1932*, second impression (A 7.2)

Colonial Press, Inc., of Clinton, Mass. The resulting book was somewhat reduced in size – the text measures 6 1/4 (6 7/16) × 4 – and in other respects the second impression differed from the first in the following ways:

Title page: The publisher's imprint at the bottom of the page was altered to read, 'UNIVERSITY OF CALIFORNIA PRESS | *Berkeley and Los Angeles 1965*'.

Collation: Same for the first impression: [unsigned, 1–14¹⁶]. However, the plates were imposed so as to leave an additional blank leaf at the beginning of the book and one less at the end, with the resulting difference in pagination: prp. 2 pp. [i–iv] v–xiii . . . 415–426 [427–428].

Contents: p. [ii]: a black and white photograph (7 3/8 × 5 3/8) of Hart Crane and, at bottom, the note, 'Photo by William Wright, 1931'. p. [iv]: 'COPYRIGHT, 1952, BY BROM WEBER | *All rights reserved* | *First California Paperbound Edition, 1965* | MANUFACTURED IN THE UNITED STATES OF AMERICA'.

Illustration: The photograph provided on p. [ii] of the second impression took the place of the deleted frontispiece of the first impression.

Typography: The inverted letter heading on p. 121 was corrected, as were the misplaced footnotes on pp. 197 and 294; there were many minor alterations and corrections of the text.

Paper: White, wove, unwatermarked. Leaves bulk 13/16; leaf thickness .0035.

Binding: Of the 6,000 copies made in the second impression, 1,000 were bound in cloth and 5,000 in paper.

Cloth binding. Light blue cloth. Front and back covers: plain. Spine: reading horizontally, all printed in black, '*The* | *Letters* | *of* HART CRANE | WEBER | California'. White, wove, unwatermarked endpapers. Top, fore-edge, and tail cut.

Paperback binding. Front cover: on a brown and white photograph of Hart Crane, at bottom left, in red, '$2.25', and at bottom right, in red, '*The Letters* | *of HART* | *CRANE* | *1916–1932* | *Edited by BROM WEBER*'. Spine: on a white background, reading horizontally, all in brown except as noted, '*The* | *Letters* | *of* | *Hart* | *Crane* | [asterisk, in red] | *WEBER*' and, at bottom, in red, 'Cal 113'. Back cover: on a white background, a descriptive note on the contents followed by quotations from reviews by Horace Gregory (*New York Tribune Book Review*, November

9, 1952) and Elizabeth Hardwick (*Partisan Review,* November–December 1953); at bottom left, in red, 'University of California Press | *Berkeley 94720*'. Top, fore-edge, and tail cut; cover cut flush.

Dust jacket (for cloth-bound books): Light blue laid paper. Front: on a background consisting of a black and light blue halftone photograph of Hart Crane, Lettered at lower right, in light blue, '*The* | *Letters* | *of* | *HART* | *CRANE* | *1916–1932* | *Edited by BROM WEBER*'. Spine: reading horizontally, '*The* | *Letters* | *of* | *Hart* | *Crane* | [asterisk] | *WEBER*' and, at bottom, '*California*'. Back: advertisements of Stephen Spender's *The Struggle of the Modern* and Blake Nevius's *Edith Wharton*. Front and rear flaps: brief description of contents, followed by quotations from reviews by Horace Gregory, Elizabeth Hardwick, and W. T. Scott, and concluding with identifications of the editor and the source of the cover picture.

Notes: Publication. The clothbound and paperback forms of the second impression were published simultaneously in September 1965. The cataloguing date of the Library of Congress copy was October 6, 1965.

Notes to section A 7: Library of Congress copyright deposit. PS3505.R272Z54 (first impression).

> *Copies examined.*
> HM: ALA 1516.15 (first impression, rebound)
> IC: B/C853 (second impression, clothbound, four copies)
> ICU: PS3506/.R2128/A3 (first impression, rebound)
> ICU: PS3506/.R2128/A31/MoPo (second impression, clothbound)
> IU: B/C8915C11 (first impression)
> IU: B/C8915C11/1965 (second impression, clothbound)
> NAlU: PS/3505/R272/Z54/1965 (second impression, clothbound)
> NAlU: PS/3505/R272/Z54/1965/cop. 2 (second impression, paperback)
> NBu: PS/3505/R2715Z54 (first impression, rebound)
> NBuU: Poetry Room (first impression, dust jacket)
> NBuU: Poetry Room (second impression, clothbound, dust jacket)
> NBuU: PS/3505/.R272Z54/1965 (second impression, clothbound)
> NJam: B/C8911 (first impression, dust jacket)
> OCl: 811.5925/253 (first impression)

WSupU: PS3505/.R272Z54/1965 (second impression, clothbound)

Personal copy of Brom Weber: (first impression, rebound;
contains pasted-in corrections and revisions and was the
copy photographed to produce the plates used for the
second impression)

Personal copies of the compilers: (second impressions, paperback)

A 8 VOYAGES

Title page: VOYAGES SIX POEMS FROM WHITE BUILD-
INGS | BY HART CRANE WITH WOOD ENGRAVINGS BY |
LEONARD BASKIN PUBLISHED BY THE MUSEUM | OF
MODERN ART NEW YORK CITY MCMLVII [The words
VOYAGES and *MCMLVII* are in red.]

Collation: (9 1/2 × 11): [unsigned, 1¹⁴], 14 leaves, pp. [1–28].

Contents: pp. [1]–[2]: blank. p. [3]: half title, '[in green]
VOYAGES | SIX POEMS BY HART CRANE'. p. [4]: blank. p.
[5]: title page. p. [6]: blank. p. [7]: headed 'I' with text. p. [8]:
headed 'II' with text. p. [9]: concluding five lines of poem II.
p. [10]: headed 'III' with text. p. [11]: blank. p. [12]: headed
'IV' with text. p. [13]: concluding twelve lines of poem IV. pp.
[14–15]: blank. p. [16]: headed 'V' with text. p. [17]: concluding
twelve lines of poem V. p. [18]: headed 'VI' with text. p. [19]:
concluding sixteen lines of poem VI. p. [20]: blank. p. [21]:
'This book, the second of a series of limited editions published
by The Museum | of Modern Art under the direction of Monroe
Wheeler has been designed, illus- | trated and printed by Leonard
Baskin at The Gehenna Press, Northampton, Mass. | in Novem-
ber, 1957. The poems have been reprinted by permission of the
Liv- | eright Publishing Corporation from "Collected Poems of
Hart Crane." The | Perpetua type has been set by hand. The il-
lustrations have been printed from | six original boxwood en-
gravings and one cherry woodcut on Amalfi Italian | hand-made
paper and on Moriki and Mending Tissue, both hand-made in
Japan. | The edition is limited to 975 numbered copies and 25
lettered review copies, | all signed by Mr. Baskin. This is copy
number'. p. [22]: blank. p. [23]: publisher's device, a 2 1/4 ×
1 1/16 orange rectangle containing the image of a bird and, immediately to the right of the rectangle the identification, 'THE
GEHENNA PRESS'. pp. [24–28]: blank.

Illustrations: Seven wood engravings, three printed with the
text and four on separate sheets tipped in.
   Engravings in the text occur as follows, all in black and
white:
   1. p. [5], to the left of the text, a figure (8 7/16 × 3 5/16) rep-
      resenting a human face and torso.
   2. p. [9], beneath the text, a figure (4 9/16 × 4 1/2) mostly
      lines and swirl patterns.
   3. p. [17], to the right of the text, a figure (5 1/2 × 2 3/8) rep-
      resenting a bird.

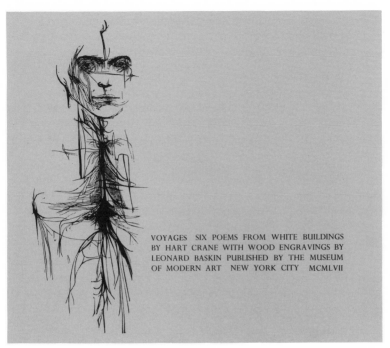

VOYAGES   SIX POEMS FROM WHITE BUILDINGS
BY HART CRANE WITH WOOD ENGRAVINGS BY
LEONARD BASKIN PUBLISHED BY THE MUSEUM
OF MODERN ART   NEW YORK CITY   MCMLVII

Title page of *Voyages* (A 8)

Engravings on separate sheets tipped in occur as follows:

1. between pp. [6] and [7], a white tissue sheet (9 17/32 × 11): verso blank; recto with an engraving (9 1/4 × 4 3/4) in orange; tipped in by sewing wraparound and by gluing to the inner edge of leaf 11.
2. between pp. [10] and [11], a sheet (8 3/8 × 11) of green, laid paper (chain lines spaced variably, from 1 3/8 to 1 1/2): verso blank; recto with a circular engraving (diameter 5 1/2) in black; tipped in by gluing at the top edge of leaf 6.
3. between pp. [14] and [15], a folded white tissue sheet (unfolded dimensions 17 1/8 × 20 1/2, folded dimensions 8 9/16 × 20 1/2), containing a rectangular engraving (4 11/32 × 15 7/8) in black and white; tipped in by gluing along the top of pp. [14] and [15].
4. between pp. [18] and [19], a white tissue sheet (9 17/32 × 11): recto with an engraving (4 7/8 × 4 1/8) in dark green; verso with an engraving (4 1/8 × 4 7/8) in light green; tipped in by gluing to the inner edge of leaf 10.

Typography: 8 1/2 × 8 5/8 (text and woodcuts). Title in 84-pt. Perpetua; subtitle in 24-pt. Perpetua; text in 14-pt. Perpetua with 6-pt. leading.

Paper: White, laid (chain lines spaced 1 1/16, running vertically), watermarked 'AMALFI'. Leaves (including tipped-in illustrations) bulk 3/32; leaf thickness varies from .0027 to .0047.

Binding: Bound by hand in a plain bluish gray heavy paper wrapper by a double stitch of gray thread through the single gathering and tied outside along the spine. Front cover has a pasted slip (1 1/8 × 5 1/4) with the wording, '[in red] VOYAGES SIX POEMS BY HART CRANE | WOOD ENGRAVINGS BY LEONARD BASKIN | THE MUSEUM OF MODERN ART MCMLVII'. Top cut, fore-edge and tail deckle edge. Fitted in a cardboard folding case covered with blue gray paper and, on the topmost folding cover, the same slip as is pasted on the wrapper.

Notes: Printing and publication. *Voyages* was set by hand, printed from standing type by Leonard Baskin at the Gehenna Press, Northampton, Mass., in an impression of 1,000 copies, and published by the Museum of Modern Art in November 1957. The Library of Congress copy was catalogued on April 10, 1958.

Numbering and signing. Copies were numbered and signed in brown ink on p. [21] immediately after the words, 'This is copy number'.

Library of Congress copyright deposit.   PS3505.R272W53.

Copies examined.
HM: Typ 970.57.3035
ICN: Wing/ZP/983/.B295
ICN: Wood Blocks/Wing/ZP/983/.B2951 (woodcut blocks
       used to print *Voyages;* the gift of Leonard Baskin)
ICU: PS3506/.R21V7/MoPo
IEN: Rare Book Room LAm/Cr (a defective copy with leaf 1
       lacking and leaf 14 loose)
NBu: Rare Book Room
NN: *KP (Gehenna) Crane
OCl: q811.5/C8497v
WMM: Rare Book Room
Personal copy of the compilers

A 9 THE COMPLETE POEMS OF HART CRANE
Third edition

Title page: The | Complete Poems | of Hart Crane | *Edited by*
Waldo Frank | DOUBLEDAY ANCHOR BOOKS | DOUBLEDAY
& COMPANY, INC. | GARDEN CITY, NEW YORK | 1958

Collation: (7 1/8 × 4 1/8): 100 leaves, pp. [i–iv] v [vi] vii–xvi
[1–2] 3–62 [63–64] 65–114 [115–116] 117–143 [144–146]
147–163 [164–166] 167–176 [177–178] 179–183 [184].

Contents: p. [i]: 'The Complete Poems of Hart Crane'. p. [ii]:
blank. p. [iii]: title page. p. [iv]: 'COVER BY ANTONIO FRAS-
CONI | TYPOGRAPHY BY EDWARD GOREY | Clothbound edi-
tions of *The Complete Poems* | *of Hart Crane* are available from
Liveright | Publishing Corp., New York | Copyright © 1933,
1958 | Liveright Publishing Corp. | Printed in the United States
of America | All Rights Reserved'. p. v: headed 'EDITOR's NOTE'
followed by text of note. p. [vi]: blank. pp. vii–x: table of contents. pp. xi–xvi: foreword by Waldo Frank, dated June 1957. p.
[1]: 'ONE | The Bridge | *From going to and fro in the earth,* |
and from walking up and down in it. | THE BOOK OF JOB'. p.
[2]: blank. pp. 3–62: text of "The Bridge." p. [63]: 'TWO |
White Buildings | TO WALDO FRANK | *Ce ne peut être que la*
fin du monde, en avançant. | RIMBAUD'. p. [64]: blank. pp.
65–114: text of "White Buildings." p. [115]: 'THREE | Key West:
| An Island Sheaf | *The starry floor,* | *The wat'ry shore,* | *Is*
given thee 'til the break of day. | BLAKE'. p. [116]: blank. pp.
117–143: text of "Key West: An Island Sheaf." p. [144]: blank.
p. [145]: 'FOUR | Uncollected Poems'. p. [146]: blank. pp.
147–163: text of "Uncollected Poems." p. [164]: blank. p. [165]:
'APPENDIX A | Early Poems'. p. [166]: headed 'Note', followed
by a twelve-line note, and signed, 'EDITOR'. pp. 167–176: text
of "Appendix A." p. [177]: 'APPENDIX B | Modern Poetry: | An
Essay'. p. [178]: blank. pp. 179–183: text of "Modern Poetry."
p. [184]: blank.

Typography: 33 ll., 5 1/4 (5 3/4) × 3 5/16. Text in 10-pt. Caledonia on 13-pt. body; running titles (e.g., 'THE BRIDGE') in
10-pt. Caledonia. Title on title page in 30-pt. Perpetua; major
division titles (e.g., p. [1]: 'The Bridge') in 24-pt. Perpetua. Page
numbers centered at foot of page.

Paper: White, wove, unwatermarked. Leaves bulk 7/16; leaf
thickness .0038.

The
Complete Poems
of Hart Crane

Edited by Waldo Frank

DOUBLEDAY ANCHOR BOOKS

DOUBLEDAY & COMPANY, INC.

GARDEN CITY, NEW YORK

1958

Title page of the third edition of *The Complete Poems of Hart Crane* (A 9)

Binding: Paperback. Cover front, spine, and back decorated with a stylized representation of a suspension bridge, buildings, birds, and ships, in black, blue, rust, and magenta. Front cover: in upper left, '*A 128*'; in upper right, '[in rust] *$1.10 in Canada.*' and '*95c*'; beneath, '[in rust] THE COMPLETE | [in rust] POEMS OF | HART CRANE'; and, at bottom, the figure of an anchor surmounted by a 'D', the shank entwined by a dolphin, in rust, above the words, '*A Doubleday Anchor Book*'. Spine: reading vertically, 'THE COMPLETE [in rust] POEMS OF [in magenta] HART CRANE' | and, at bottom, horizontally, '[all in rust] *Anchor | A | 128*'. Back cover: '[in magenta] THE COMPLETE POEMS OF | HART CRANE' followed by an eight-line statement on the editing, scope, and availability of a hard-bound edition of the volume and, beneath, in magenta, the figure of an anchor surmounted by a 'D', the shank entwined by a dol-phin, and to the right of this device, '[in magenta] *A Doubleday Anchor* Book'; at bottom right, the signature 'Frasconi'. All edges cut; cover cut flush.

Notes: Publication. Copyright application records show that this paperback edition was published by Doubleday & Company in its Anchor Book series on January 16, 1958. Printing and binding was done at the Doubleday & Company plant in Han-over, Pennsylvania. The Library of Congress copy was cata-logued on December 23, 1957. Four impressions were made for a total of 55,000 copies, of which 51,724 copies were sold before the book went out of print. All impressions were made from rubber plates. *The Complete Poems of Hart Crane* was adver-tised by Doubleday in *Publishers' Weekly* of March 18, 1957, as ready in January. The notation on p. [iv], "Clothbound edi-tions of *The Complete Poems of Hart Crane* are available from Liveright Publishing Corp., New York," refers to the Black & Gold printing of *The Collected Poems of Hart Crane* published by Liveright in 1946. The text follows that of the first edition of *The Collected Poems of Hart Crane,* 1933, but with a shorter introduction specially prepared by Waldo Frank for this edition and dated June 1957.

Library of Congress copyright deposit. PS3505.R272 1958.

Copies examined.
British Museum: 011421.52
Personal copies of the compilers

A 10 THE COMPLETE POEMS AND SELECTED
LETTERS AND PROSE OF HART CRANE

A 10.1
First impression

Title page: THE | COMPLETE POEMS | AND SELECTED
LETTERS | AND PROSE OF | [rule 2 3/4] | HART CRANE |
[rule 2 3/4] | EDITED WITH AN | INTRODUCTION AND
NOTES BY | BROM WEBER | ANCHOR BOOKS | DOUBLE-
DAY & COMPANY, INC. | GARDEN CITY, NEW YORK

Collation: (7 1/4 × 4 5/32): 160 leaves, pp. [i–vi] vii–xvii
[xviii] [1–2] 3–41 [42–44] 45–46 [47] 48–52 [53] 54–79 [80–
81] 82–85 [86–87] 88–95 [96–97] 98–102 [103] 104–106 [107]
108–112 [113] 114–117 [118–121] 122–152 [153–155] 156–174
[175] 176–194 [195–196] 197–266 [267–268] 269–302.

Contents: p. [i]: 'THE | COMPLETE POEMS | AND SE-
LECTED LETTERS | AND PROSE OF | HART CRANE | [oval
device containing the figure of an anchor and the letters 'D',
'A', and 'B']'. p. [ii]: blank. p. [iii]: title page. p. [iv]: 'Some of
the material collected in the present edition | and used by per-
mission of the Hart Crane Estate was | first published in book
form as follows:' with sources cited beneath in three paragraphs (totaling eleven lines), followed by, 'The publishers wish
to thank Samuel Loveman for | his assistance and co-operation.
| [space] | *The Complete Poems and Selected Letters and Prose
| of Hart Crane* was originally published in a hard- | bound
edition by Liveright Publishing Corp. in 1966. | The Anchor
Books edition is published by arrange- | ment with Liveright
Publishing Corp. | [space] | Anchor Books edition: 1966', fol-
lowed by notice of availability of hardbound copies (totaling
three lines) and concluding, '*The Letters of Hart Crane, 1916–
1932*, Copyright | 1952 by Brom Weber | Copyright © 1933, 1958,
1966 by Liveright Publish- | ing Corp. | Printed in the United
States of America | All Rights Reserved'. p. [v]: '*To Waldo Frank
| Constant Friend of Hart Crane*'. p. [vi]: blank. pp. vii–x:
table of contents. pp. xi–xvii: introduction by Brom Weber. p.
[xviii]: blank. p. [1]: 'ONE | [rule (2 25/32)] | White Buildings
| [rule (2 25/32)] | TO WALDO FRANK | *Ce ne peut être que la
fin du monde, en avançant.* | RIMBAUD'. p. [2]: blank. pp. 3–
41: text of "White Buildings." p. [42]: blank. p. [43]: 'TWO |
[rule (2 25/32)] | The Bridge | [rule (2 25/32)] | *From going to
and fro in the earth, | and from walking up and down in it.* |

THE

COMPLETE POEMS

AND SELECTED LETTERS

AND PROSE OF

HART CRANE

EDITED WITH AN

INTRODUCTION AND NOTES BY

BROM WEBER

ANCHOR BOOKS

DOUBLEDAY & COMPANY, INC.

GARDEN CITY, NEW YORK

Title page of *The Complete Poems and Selected Letters and Prose of Hart Crane,* first impression (A 10.1)

THE BOOK OF JOB'. p. [44]: blank. pp. 45–117: text of "The Bridge." p. [118]: blank. p. [119]: 'THREE | [rule (2 25/32)] | Uncollected Poems | [rule (2 25/32)]'. p. [120]: blank. p. [121]: 'I | Early Poems'. pp. 122–152: text. p. [153]: 'II | Late Poems'. p. [154]: blank. p. [155]: 'Key West: | An Island Sheaf | *The Starry floor,* | *The wat'ry shore,* | *Is given thee 'til the break of day.* | BLAKE'. pp. 156–174: text. p. [175]: 'III | More Late Poems'. pp. 176–194: text. p. [195]: 'FOUR | [rule (2 25/32)] | Selected Prose | [rule (2 25/32)]'. p. [196]: blank. pp. 197–266: text. p. [267]: 'APPENDIX | Hart Crane, by Waldo Frank'. p. [268]: blank. pp. 269–273: text. p. 274–295: notes. pp. 296–298: index to first lines. pp. 299–302: index to titles.

Items included: Introduction; WHITE BUILDINGS; Black Tambourine; Emblems of Conduct; My Grandmother's Love Letters; Sunday Morning Apples; Praise for an Urn; Garden Abstract; Stark Major; Chaplinesque; Pastorale; In Shadow; The Fernery; North Labrador; Repose of Rivers; Paraphrase; Possessions; Lachrymae Christi; Passage; The wine Menagerie; Recitative; For the Marriage of Faustus and Helen I, II, III; At Melville's Tomb; Voyages I, II, III, IV, V, VI; THE BRIDGE; To Brooklyn Bridge; Ave Maria; Powhatan's Daughter; The Harbor Dawn; Van Winkle; The River; The Dance; Indiana; Cutty Sark; Cape Hatteras; Three Songs; Southern Cross; National Winter Garden; Virginia; Quaker Hill; The Tunnel; Atlantis; UNCOLLECTED POEMS; EARLY POEMS; The Moth that God Made Blind; C33; October-November; The Hive; Fear; Annunciations; Echoes; The Bathers; Modern Craft; Carmen de Boheme; Carrier Letter; Post script; Forgetfulness; To Portapovitch; Legende; Interior; Episode of Hands; The Bridge at Estador; Porphyro in Akron; A Persuasion; Locutions des Pierrots; The Great Western Plains; America's Plutonic Ecstasies; Interludium; LATE POEMS; KEY WEST: AN ISLAND SHEAF; O Carib Isle!; The Mermen; To the Cloud Juggler; The Mango Tree; Island Quarry; Old Song; The Idiot; A Name for All; Bacardi Spreads the Eagle's Wings; Imperator Victus; Royal Palm; The Air Plant; The Hurricane; To Emily Dickinson; Key West; −And Bees of Paradise; Moment Fugue; By Nilus Once I Knew . . . ; MORE LATE POEMS; The Visible the Untrue; Reply; The Phantom Bark; Lenses; To Liberty; Eternity; To the Empress Josephine's Statue; A Postscript; To Shakespeare; March; Havana Rose; Reliquary; Purgatorio; The Sad Indian; The Broken Tower; SELECTED PROSE; The Case Against Nietzsche; Joyce and Ethics; Review of The Ghetto and Other Poems; Review of Minna and Myself; Review of Winesburg,

Ohio; A Note on Minns; Sherwood Anderson; Review of Eight More Harvard Poets; General Aims and Theories; A Letter to Gorham Munson; A Letter to Waldo Frank; A Letter to Harriet Monroe; A Letter to Yvor Winters; A Letter to Otto H. Kahn; A Letter to Herbert Weinstock; A Letter to Allen Tate; Modern Poetry; From Haunts of Proserpine; Hart Crane, by Waldo Frank; Notes; Index of First Lines; Index of Titles.

The following poems appear in this edition but not in *Collected Poems*, 1933 and 1938, or *Complete Poems*, 1958: "The Moth that God Made Blind," "C33," "Echoes," "Carmen de Boheme," "Legende," "Interior," "Episode of Hands," "The Bridge of Estador," "Porphyro in Akron," "A Persuasion," "Locutions des Pierrots," "The Great Western Plains," "America's Plutonic Ecstasies," "Interludium," "Lenses," "To Liberty," and "To the Empress Josephine's Statue."

Typography: 36 ll., 5 7/8 (6 1/16) × 3 9/32. Introduction and text in 10-pt. Linotype Electra set on 12-pt. body. Page numbers centered at foot of type page. The italic glosses for "The Bridge" were printed on separate pages facing the text (e.g., pp. 48–49) for reasons explained by Brom Weber in his "Introduction," pp. xvi–xvii:

> The position of the glosses in *The Bridge* was of great importance to Crane. Because the size of the page in the paperback edition did not permit of placing them on the same page, I have adopted the expedient of putting them on the facing page (either right or left, as Crane indicated) so that the reader may see them exactly where Crane intended them to be. Although this arrangement results in a certain amount of blank space which did not appear in the original edition, it does give a greater fidelity to the original than was possible in the previous paperback edition.

Paper: White, wove, unwatermarked. Leaves bulk 5/8; leaf thickness .0039.

Binding: Paperback. Front cover: top left, '[in red] A537', top right '[in red] $1.45', and beneath, '[in red] THE COMPLETE POEMS | [in red] AND SELECTED LETTERS | [in red] AND PROSE OF | [lettered in black outline] HART CRANE | [reproduction of a painting, predominately in reds, blues, and greens, of a suspension bridge pillars and cables] | [in red] A Doubleday Anchor Book', and, at bottom right, in red, an oval device containing the figure of an anchor and the letters 'D', 'A', and 'B'. Spine: at top, reading vertically, all in red, 'THE COMPLETE POEMS | AND SELECTED LETTERS | AND PROSE OF';

below, lettered in black outline, 'HART CRANE' with a continuation of the front cover painting beneath; and, at bottom,
reading horizontally, 'Anchor | A537' in red. Back cover: '[at
top left] POETRY | [in red] THE COMPLETE POEMS AND
SELECTED LETTERS | [in red] AND PROSE OF | [lettered in
black outline] HART CRANE | [in red] *Edited with an Intro-
duction and Notes* | [in red] *by Brom Weber*', followed by a de-
scription of the contents, a note identifying Brom Weber, and
an indication of the availability of a hardbound edition (totaling
fourteen lines of text); beneath, a continuation of the painting
from the front cover and spine; at bottom, all in red, 'COVER
BY JIM VAN DIJK | A Doubleday Anchor Book'; and, at right
bottom, in red, an oval device identical with that on the front
cover.

*Notes: Publication. The Complete Poems and Selected Let-
ters and Prose of Hart Crane* was printed from rubber plates
and bound at the Doubleday & Company plant in Hanover, Pennsylvania. The copyright application shows the date of publication as September 16, 1966. The Library of Congress copy was
catalogued on October 13, 1966. Thirty thousand and seventy-
eight copies were printed, with sales of 20,908 as of March 1969.

A 10.2
Second impression: In September 1966 a clothbound edition
of *The Complete Poems and Selected Letters and Prose of Hart
Crane* was published by the Liveright Publishing Corporation;
the Library of Congress copy was catalogued on November 7,
1966. This impression of 5,950 copies was made from lithographic plates obtained by photographic enlargement of proofs
printed from the Doubleday & Company Anchor Book plates.
The enlargement yielded a text page 6 3/4 (7 1/32) × 3 3/4, and a
text-type size equivalent to 12-pt. Other differences are as follows:

Title page: THE COMPLETE POEMS | AND SELECTED
LETTERS | AND PROSE OF | [hollow letter] HART CRANE |
Edited with an Introduction and Notes | *by Brom Weber* | [two
vine and leaf devices arranged with curled stems toward one
another and, pointing outward along each stem, the same ar-
rangement of five leaves] | [rule (3 27/32)] | LIVERIGHT PUB-
LISHING CORPORATION | NEW YORK

Collation: (8 5/16 × 5 1/2): [unsigned, 1–10¹⁶]. Number of
leaves and pagination identical with paperback edition.

Contents: p. [i]: half title. p. [ii]: black and white photograph
(5 7/16 × 3 3/4) of a portrait of Hart Crane and, beneath, the no-

**THE COMPLETE POEMS
AND SELECTED LETTERS
AND PROSE OF**

HART CRANE

*Edited with an Introduction and Notes
by Brom Weber*

LIVERIGHT PUBLISHING CORPORATION

NEW YORK

Title page of *The Complete Poems and Selected Letters and Prose of Hart Crane,* second impression (A 10.2)

tation, 'HART CRANE | *From a portrait by David Alfaro Si-queiros*'. p. [iii]: title page. p. [iv]: 'Copyright © 1933, 1958, 1966 by Liveright Publish- | ing Corp. | *The Letters of Hart Crane, 1916–1932*, Copyright | 1952 by Brom Weber', followed by list of sources used by permission and concluding, 'The publishers wish to thank Samuel Loveman for | his assistance and co-operation. | Printed in the United States of America | All Rights Reserved | Library of Congress Catalog Card No. 66–19992'. p. [v]: *'To Waldo Frank | Constant Friend of Hart Crane'.* p. [vi]: blank. pp. vii–x: table of contents. pp. xi–xvii: introduction by Brom Weber. p. [xviii]: blank. p. [1]: 'ONE | [rule (3 3/16)] | White Buildings | [rule (3 3/16)] | TO WALDO FRANK | *Ce ne peut être que la fin du monde, en avançant.* | RIMBAUD'. p. [2]: black and white photograph (6 9/16 × 4 3/8) and, beneath, the caption, 'HART CRANE | From a photograph by Walker Evans'.

Paper: White, wove, unwatermarked. Leaves bulk 7/8; leaf thickness .0051.

Binding: Diagonal fine rib-cloth (S), black, with lettering, rules, and fleurons, all stamped in gilt; all edges cut. In general the binding is consistent with other volumes in the Black & Gold Library series. Front cover: a facsimile of Hart Crane's signature, stamped in gilt. Spine, from the top: a band of arabesque fleurons (1/2) bordered by a double rule above and a single rule below; a red band (1 1/2) bordered at top and bottom by thick rules (1/16) and stamped, reading horizontally, 'COMPLETE | POEMS | [small ornament] | SELECTED LETTERS | AND PROSE OF | HART | CRANE'; a narrow red band (1/16); single rules spaced 5 1/4 apart and enclosing ten bands of arabesque fleurons (each 1/2); a red band (5/16) bordered at top and bottom by thick rules (1/16) and stamped 'LIVERIGHT'; a band of arabesque fleurons (1/2) bordered by a single rule above and a double rule below. Back cover: plain. White, wove, unwatermarked endpapers.

Dust jacket: White background. Front cover: light blue diagonal borders left and right; near top center, a sepia-tone photograph (4 × 2 13/16) of a portrait of Hart Crane, irregularly bordered in black on the left side and bottom; and below, the wording, 'The | [in red] COMPLETE POEMS | and | [in red] Selected Letters and Prose of | [in blue] HART CRANE | Edited with an Introduction by BROM WEBER'. Spine: all reading horizontally, 'The | [in red] COMPLETE | [in red] POEMS | and | [in red] Selected | [in red] Letters | [in red] and | [in red] Prose | of |

[sepia-tone photograph (1 5/16 × 1) of a portrait of Hart Crane] | [in blue] HART | [in blue] CRANE | LIVERIGHT'. Back cover: listing of the Living Books in Psychology series. Front flap: at top right, '[all in red] BLACK & GOLD EDITION | 320 Pages $5.50', followed below by indication of title, author, and editor; beneath, a publisher's note beginning, "This is the most complete and authoritative collection of the works of Hart Crane ever published," and ending, "For Crane, the imposing, cold steel of a monumental bridge spanned the separated shores of matter and mind, and linked man-made machines with the human spirit"; and, at bottom, credits for jacket illustrations. Rear flap: at top, indications of edition, pages, price, title, author, and editor exactly as for front flap; beneath, quotations of critical comments by the *New York Herald Tribune*, Eugene O'Neill, *Poetry Magazine*, the *New York Evening Post*, Malcolm Cowley, and the *London Times;* and at bottom, publisher's address and ordering information.

Notes: Publication. The number of copies printed is undisclosed.

A 10.3
Third impression: In September 1968 Oxford University Press published *The Complete Poems and Selected Letters and Prose of Hart Crane* using lithographic plates derived from the Liveright Publishing Corporation impression. One thousand five hundred copies were printed by photo-offset; these differed from the Liveright impression in the following ways:

Title page: THE COMPLETE POEMS | AND SELECTED LETTERS | AND PROSE OF | [hollow letter] HART CRANE | *Edited with an Introduction and Notes* | *by Brom Weber* | [rule (3 13/16)] | LONDON | OXFORD UNIVERSITY PRESS | 1968

Collation: (8 7/16 × 5 7/16): [unsigned, 1–20⁸]. Number of leaves and pagination identical with Liveright impression.

Contents: Identical with the Liveright impression except for the following: p. [ii]: black and white photograph of Hart Crane (6 3/8 × 4 1/4) and, beneath, the notation, 'HART CRANE | *From a photograph by Walker Evans*'. p. [iv]: *'Oxford University Press, Ely House, London W. 1* | GLASGOW NEW YORK TORONTO MELBOURNE WELLINGTON | CAPE TOWN SALISBURY IBADAN NAIROBI LUSAKA ADDIS ABABA | BOMBAY CALCUTTA MADRAS KARACHI LAHORE DACCA | KUALA LUMPUR HONG KONG TOKYO | Copy-

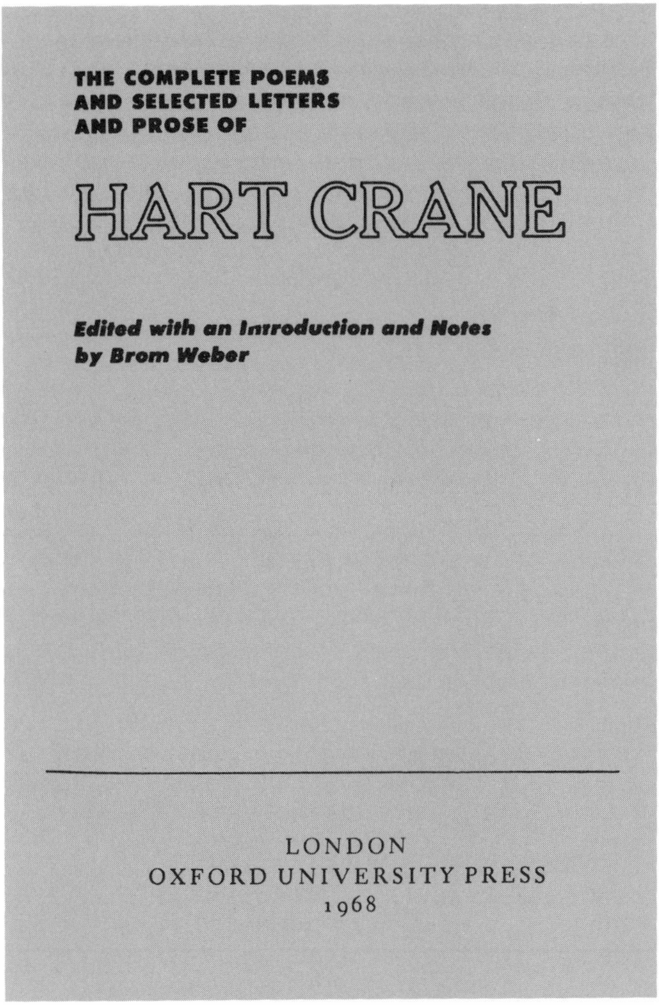

THE COMPLETE POEMS
AND SELECTED LETTERS
AND PROSE OF

HART CRANE

*Edited with an Introduction and Notes
by Brom Weber*

LONDON
OXFORD UNIVERSITY PRESS
1968

Title page of *The Complete Poems and Selected Letters and
Prose of Hart Crane*, third impression (A 10.3)

right © 1933, 1958, 1966 by Liveright Publish- | ing Corp. | *The Letters of Hart Crane,* 1916–1932, Copyright | 1952 by Brom Weber | Reprinted lithographically in Great Britain by | Latimer Trend & Co., Ltd., Whitstable'. p. [vi]: headed 'AC-KNOWLEDGEMENTS' and, beneath, the statement, 'Some of the material collected in the present edition | and used by permission of the Hart Crane Estate was | first published in book form as follows:', followed by a list of three book titles and concluding with the statement, 'The publishers wish to thank Samuel Loveman for | his assistance and co-operation.'.

Paper: White, wove, unwatermarked. Leaves bulk 13/16; leaf thickness .005.

Binding: Calico cloth (V), dull black. Front cover: plain. Spine: reading horizontally, from the top, all stamped in gilt, '[device consisting of one thick and one thin rule (1 1/8) with ends joined by short curved rules (1/4) extending downward from the thick rule and 1/8 beyond the end of the thin rule] | The | Complete | Poems | and | Selected | Letters | and Prose | of | HART | CRANE | [device consisting of one thin and one thick rule (1 1/8) with ends joined by short curved rules (1/4) extending upward from the thick rule and 1/8 beyond the end of the thin rule]' and, at bottom, 'OXFORD'. Back cover: plain. White, wove, unwatermarked endpapers. Top, fore-edge, and tail cut.

Dust jacket: Front cover: top third, in white, on a green background, 'The Complete Poems | & Selected Letters | & Prose | [rule (5 1/4)] | HART CRANE'; bottom two-thirds, a brown-and-orange-tone photograph (6 1/4 × 5 7/8) of Hart Crane, having at bottom, in white, the note, 'Edited with an Introduction | and Notes by Brom Weber'. Spine: on a green background, reading horizontally from the top, in white, '[rule (1 1/4)] | The | Complete | Poems | and | Selected | Letters | and Prose | of | HART | CRANE [rule (1 1/4)]' and, at bottom, 'Oxford'. Back cover: on an orange background, advertisements of other Oxford University Press books. Front flap: on a white background, two paragraphs of comment on Crane's poetry and, at bottom, '42s. net | IN UK ONLY'. Back flap: plain.

Notes to section A 10: *Library of Congress copyright deposit.* PS3505.R272 1966 (first impression).

Copies examined.
HM: ALA 1516.3 (second impression)
IC: 821/C85A2 (second impression, two copies)
ICU: PS3506/.R21/1966/MoPo (second impression)

IU: 811/C847/1966a (first impression)
IU: 811/C847/1966 (second impression)
Liveright Publishing Corporation library (second impression)
NAlU: PS/3505/R272/1966a (first impression)
NBu: PS/3505/R2715A2 (second impression)
NBuU: PS/3505/.R272/1966 (first impression)
NBuU: Poetry Room (second impression, dust jacket)
NBuU: Poetry Room (third impression, dust jacket, two
        copies)
WMM: 818.5/C85co (second impression)
WSupU: 811.5/C85co (first impression)
WSupU: PS3505/R272/1966a (second impression)
Personal copies of the compilers: (first impression, two copies;
        third impression, with dust jackets, two copies)

A 11 SEVEN LYRICS

Title page: HART CRANE | [swelled rule (2 1/2)] | SEVEN
LYRICS | THE IBEX PRESS

Collation: (8 5/16 × 7): [unsigned, 1¹²], 12 leaves, pp. [1–24].

Contents: pp. [1–3]: blank. p. [4]: engraving by Laurence
Scott. p. [5]: title page. p. [6]: '© Copyright, 1966 by Kenneth
A. Lohf'. pp. [7–9]: preface by Kenneth A. Lohf. p. [10]: blank.
p. [11]: 'NAIAD OF MEMORY' and text of poem (totaling eleven
lines). p. [12]: 'TO EARTH' and text of poem (totaling four
lines). p. [13]: 'EXILE | (*after the Chinese*)' and text of poem
(totaling eight lines). p. [14]: 'LOVE AND A LAMP' and text of
poem totaling twelve lines). p. [15]: 'ECHOES' and text of poem
(totaling twelve lines). p. [16]: 'MEDUSA' and text of poem (totaling fourteen lines). p. [17]: 'MEDITATION' and text of poem
(totaling eighteen lines). p. [18]: blank. p. [19]: at top the head
of an ibex and, beneath, the notation: 'This edition consists of
two hundred fifty copies, of which fifty are *hors | commerce,*
printed in Cambridge, Massachusetts, January, 1966. | Frontis-
piece engraving by Laurence Scott. The Ibex Press: | Jeffrey
Kindley · Laurence Rhu · Laurence Scott | Number'. pp. [20–24]:
blank.

Typography: 25 ll. (preface) and 22 ll. (text), 6 × 5 5/8. Pref-
ace in 14-pt. Fairfield Medium with 2-pt. leading; text in 14-pt.
Fairfield Medium with 6-pt. leading; titles of poems in 14-pt.
Fairfield; title page and cover in 36-pt. Goudy Old Style.

Paper: White, laid (chain lines spaced 1 1/32, running horizontally), watermarked 'CURTIS RAG'. Leaves bulk 3/32; leaf
thickness .0066.

Binding: Bound by hand in a wrapper of stiff brown paper
sewn with the single gathering by a double stitch and folded over
the fore-edges of the first and last leaves. All edges cut; the fore-
edge was cut to form a slight concave, and the fore-edges of the
first and last leaves were cut 1/4 inch short to accommodate
the folded wrapper flaps. Wrapper front: 'HART CRANE |
[swelled rule (2 1/2)] | SEVEN LYRICS'. Wrapper back: plain.

Notes: Printing and publication. Two hundred and fifty
copies were printed from standing type and bound by Laurence
H. Scott at the Ibex Press, Cambridge, Mass., in January 1966.
The *hors commerce* copies, numbered 1 through 50, are in every
respect identical with other copies of the edition. This edition

HART CRANE

SEVEN LYRICS

THE IBEX PRESS

Title page of *Seven Lyrics* (A 11)

was not advertised, but was sold to libraries and private individuals applying to Laurence H. Scott who, with Jeffrey Kindley and Laurence Rhu, collaborated to form the Ibex Press in 1965. In the fall of 1965, Kenneth Lohf wrote to Laurence Scott offering him eight poems for printing and illustrating; seven of these were printed as *Seven Lyrics* and the eighth, *With a Photograph to Zell,* separately as a broadside.

Engraving block.   The woodcut block used in the printing of *Seven Lyrics* is owned by Laurence Scott.

Signing and numbering.   The frontispiece engraving was regularly autographed in pencil, 'Scott', and the signature of Kenneth A. Lohf usually appears in blue ink at the bottom of p. [9]. Copies were numbered in red on p. [19].

Text.   In his "Preface" to *Seven Lyrics,* Kenneth Lohf identified the poems as those which Crane had submitted, with an accompanying letter, to the Reverend Charles C. Bubb of the Church Head Press, Cleveland, in November of 1918. In his letter to the Reverend Mr. Bubb (reprinted as letter no. 15 on pp. 11–12 of Weber, *The Letters of Hart Crane*), Crane made the following comment on the poems he was submitting: "They have been published mostly in *The Pagan,* one in *The Little Review* of December last, and while they are few in number, I thought that they might possibly be equal to the boundaries of a modest pamphlet. 'Six Lyrics,' or some such title might be used for the booklet." In his letter, then, Crane seems to have been referring to previously published poems, and these, in fact, are not difficult to identify: the poem which appeared in the December 1917 issue of *The Little Review* was "In Shadow," and Crane had written eight other poems which had been published in *The Pagan* by this time, five of which, presumably, he had selected as his best, to accompany "In Shadow." Yet, of the poems printed in *Seven Lyrics,* only "Echoes" had appeared in *The Pagan,* and the rest had never before been published. It seems probable, then, that the poems printed in *Seven Lyrics* are not those to which Crane referred in his letter to the Reverend Mr. Bubb.

Copies examined.
HM: *65–1632
ICN: 4A/3297
ICU: PS3506/R21S49/1966/MoPo
IEN: Rare Book Room/Am/C891s
InNd: Rare Book Room/Pr/3505/R165s

NBuU: PS/3505/.R272S3
NBuU: Poetry Room
NN: *KP/(IBEX)/CRANE
NNC: Special Collections/B812C849/L/1966
WMM: Rare Book Room
Personal copy of compilers

A 12 WITH A PHOTOGRAPH TO ZELL, NOW
BOUND FOR SPAIN

Collation: Broadside (21 1/4 × 10 1/4).

Contents: Recto: 'With a Photograph | to Zell, now bound for
Spain | [engraving (6 1/4 × 7 5/16)] | [text of poem, totaling
twenty lines] | HART CRANE | *This poem is here printed for
the first time in a broadside edition of sixty copies at* THE
IBEX PRESS, | *February,* 1966, *at Cambridge, Massachusetts.
Engraving by Laurence Scott. All rights reserved.*' Verso:
blank.

Typography: Text in 24-pt. Goudy Old Style.

Paper: White, wove, unwatermarked; leaf thickness varies
from .0060 to .0067.

Binding: Unbound and unfolded; top and sides cut, bottom
deckle edge.

Notes: Printing and publication. Sixty copies were printed
in February 1966. The procedure for printing and distributing
these broadsides was the same as for the *Seven Lyrics* pamphlet printed a month earlier; for details, see the note on the
printing and publication of *Seven Lyrics.*

   Numbering and signing. Copies were not numbered; the
signature 'Scott' regularly appears beneath the engraving in
pencil.

   Engraving block. The woodcut block used in the printing of
With a Photograph to Zell is owned by Laurence Scott.

   Copies examined.
   HM: *pAB9/C8502/966w
   IEN: LAm/C89/wi
   NBuU: Poetry Room
   NNC: B812C849/Y53/1966
   WMM: Rare Book Room
   Personal copy of compilers

With a Photograph
to Zell, now bound for Spain

From Brooklyn Heights one sees the bay:
And, anchored at my window sill,
I've often sat and watched all day
The boats stream by against the shrill
Manhattan skyline, — endlessly
Their mastheads filing out to sea.

And just so, as you see me here
(Though kodaked somewhat out of focus
My eyes have still the proper locus)
I'm flashing greetings to your pier,
Your ship, your auto-bus in France —
All things on which you glide or prance
Down into sunny Spain, dear Zell.
Good berths, good food and wine as well!

I hope to know these wishes a true
Forecasting.   Let me hear from you.
Enclose some petals from a wall
Of roses in Castile, or maybe garden stall;
While I'll be waiting at this old address,
Dear Aunt, God-mother, Editress!

HART CRANE

This poem is here printed for the first time in a broadside edition of sixty copies at THE IBEX PRESS, February, 1966, at Cambridge, Massachusetts. Engraving by Laurence Scott. All rights reserved.

With a Photograph to Zell, Now Bound for Spain, a broad-side (A 12)

A 13 TWENTY-ONE LETTERS FROM HART
CRANE TO GEORGE BRYAN

Title page: TWENTY-ONE LETTERS | from HART CRANE |
to GEORGE BRYAN | *Edited by* | *Joseph Katz, Hugh C. Atkin-
son, and Richard A. Ploch* | Columbus | The Ohio State Univer-
sity Libraries | 1968

Collation: (9 × 6): [unsigned, 1¹⁶], 16 leaves, pp. [1–32].

Contents: p. [1]: 'TWENTY-ONE LETTERS | FROM HART
CRANE | TO GEORGE BRYAN | [swelled rule (19/32)] | THE
OHIO STATE UNIVERSITY LIBRARIES PUBLICATIONS |
NUMBER 4'. p. [2]: blank. p. [3]: title page. p. [4]: 'COPY-
RIGHT, 1968, BY THE OHIO STATE UNIVERSITY LIBRAR-
IES'. pp. [5–6]: introduction. pp. [7–32]: text.

Typography: 31 ll. (introduction), 27 ll. (text), 6 × 4 5/8. Introduction in 10-pt. Caledonia; text of letters in 10-pt. Caledonia;
title in 30-pt. Times Roman. Letters numbered in roman numerals
centered at top of type page; bibliographic information provided
in italic type.

Paper: White, laid (chain lines spaced 7/8, running vertically),
watermarked 'Beckett'. Leaves bulk 1/8; leaf thickness .0055.

Binding: Bound in tan, laid (chain lines spaced 13/16, running
vertically), heavy paper wrapper, watermarked 'Beckett', the
wrapper and single gathering stitched with two staples. Front
cover: 'TWENTY-ONE LETTERS | from HART CRANE | to
GEORGE BRYAN | *Edited by* | *Joseph Katz, Hugh C. Atkinson,
and Richard A. Ploch*'. Recto of rear cover: 'This edition con-
sists of | five hundred copies, of | which fifty, on India | Beckett
Text, are reserved | from distribution.'. Versos of front and rear
cover blank. All edges cut.

Reserved copies
Fifty copies of this edition were reserved from normal distribution. These differed from the ordinary copies in the following
ways:

Paper: Wove, unwatermarked; in contrast with the paper of
the regular copies, the paper color of the reserved copies appears
to be distinctly cream or light tan. Leaves bulk 3/32; leaf thickness .005.

TWENTY-ONE LETTERS
from HART CRANE
to GEORGE BRYAN

Edited by

Joseph Katz, Hugh C. Atkinson, and Richard A. Ploch

Columbus
The Ohio State University Libraries
1968

Title page of *Twenty-one Letters from Hart Crane to George Bryan* (A 13)

Binding: Weight, chain lines, and watermark identical with the ordinary copies; but the color is distinctly yellow.

Notes to section A 13: *Publication.* Printed from standing type set by linotype; polychrome cover printed by offset. The printing and binding were done by the Old Trail Printing Company, 1184 Lockhurst Avenue, Columbus, Ohio, the impression consisting of five hundred copies. This pamphlet was not offered for sale but was privately distributed by the Ohio State University Libraries to other libraries and private parties; the Ohio State University Library regards the publication date as February 1969. There is plainly a discrepancy between the statement printed on the recto of the rear cover of this edition about the form of reserved copies and the facts of the copies printed as described above. In a letter of January 11, 1970, one of the editors of the pamphlet, Prof. Joseph Katz of the University of South Carolina, has kindly provided an account which helps to explain the origin of this discrepancy; he writes:

> The edition was supposed to have been five hundred copies. Of those, four hundred and fifty copies were to have been on white Beckett text for distribution to the friends of the Library, and fifty copies on India Beckett text were to have been reserved for the private use of the three editors. But either publisher or printer erred: editors' copies are on a wove India paper in wrappers of laid India Beckett cover stock, while the major state is on white Beckett in laid bamboo Beckett cover stock. The limitation statement on the inside back wrapper, therefore, is wrong—it was written to describe the intended publication and the publisher did not correct it to reflect accurately the situation that developed.

Misprint. In the bibliographic note to letter XIX, the word *Postmarked* was printed as *Postparked* in all copies printed.

Text. The source of the letters is described in the introduction as follows:

> The letters are all in the Rare Book Room of the Ohio State University Libraries and were acquired through the efforts of Professor Matthew J. Bruccoli. Letter VIII, XVII, XX, and XXI saw limited circulation in *The Free Lance*, VII, 1 (1963), 3-7, before their purchase by the library. The remaining letters are first published here.

Copies examined.
NFredU: Rare Book Room (distribution form)
WMM: Rare Book Room (distribution form)
WMUW: Rare Book Room (distribution form)
Personal copies of compilers: (five copies in distribution form,
    one copy in reserved form)

B. Works Not Published Separately

Note: As page proof was being returned to the printer, it was discovered that ten previously unpublished poems will appear in *Antaeus,* 5 (Spring 1972). The first lines and approximate dates of composition of these poems, all but one (VIII) of which are untitled, follow:

I. "Dust now is the old-fashioned house" (ca. 1920)
II. "There are the local orchard boughs" (ca. 1920)
III. "You are that frail decision that devised" (ca. 1923–1926)
IV. "Her eyes had the blue of desperate days," (ca. May 1925)
V. "All this—and the housekeeper—" (ca. March 1926)
VI. "I have that sure enclitic to my act" (ca. 1926–1929)
VII. "I rob my breast to reach those altitudes—" (ca. 1928–1930)
VIII. "To Conquer Variety": "I have seen my ghost broken" (ca. 1931–1932)
IX. "Did one look at what one saw" (n.d.)
X. "They were there falling;" (ca. March–April 1932)

B 1
"Again"
See "The Wine Menagerie."

B 2
"The Air Plant"
Rejected by *Criterion;* first published in *The Dial,* 84 (February 1928), 140. Brom Weber in *Complete Poems,* 1966, incorrectly gives the date as *January* 1928. *Modern American Poetry and Modern British Poetry*, edited by Louis Untermeyer. New York: Harcourt, Brace and Company, 1930. *Collected Poems,* 1933 and 1938. *The Complete Poems,* 1958 and 1966.

First line: "This tuft that thrives on saline nothingness"

B 3
"The Alert Pillow"
Hart Crane: A Conversation With Samuel Loveman, edited by Jay Socin and Kirby Congdon. New York: Interim Books, 1964.

First line: "The alert pillow, the hay-seed spreads"

B 4
"America's Plutonic Ecstasies"
First published in *S4N,* 4 (May–August 1923), unpaged. Brom Weber, *Hart Crane.* New York: The Bodley Press, 1948. *Complete Poems,* 1966.

First line: "Preferring laxatives to wine"

B 5
"–And Bees of Paradise"
First published as "And Bees of Paradise" in *The New Republic,* 74 (February 15, 1933), 16. *Collected Poems,* 1933 and 1938. *Complete Poems,* 1958 and 1966.

First line: "I had come all the way here from the sea"

89

B 6

"Annunciations"

First published in *The Pagan*, 1-2 (April–May 1917), 11, as by "Harold H. Crane." *Collected Poems,* 1933. *Complete Poems,* 1958 and 1966.

First line: "The anxious milk-blood in the veins of the earth"

ANNUNCIATIONS

The anxious milk-blood in the veins of the earth,
That strives long and quiet to sever the girth
Of greenery....Below the roots, a quickening quiver
Aroused by some light that had sensed,—ere the shiver
Of the first moth's descent,—day's predestiny....
The sound of a dove's flight waved over the lawn....
The moans of travail of one dearest beside me....
Then high cries from great chasms of chaos outdrawn....
Hush! these things were all heard before dawn.

—Harold H. Crane.

"Annunciations," signed by "Harold H. Crane," from *The Pagan* (B 6)

B 7

"Atlantis"

American Poets: 1630–1930, edited by Mark Van Doren. Boston: Little, Brown & Co., 1932. *The Bridge,* 1930, both editions. *Collected Poems,* 1933 and 1938. *Complete Poems,* 1958 and 1966.

First line: "Through the bound cable strands, the arching path"

B 8

"At Melville's Tomb"

First published in *The Calendar* (London), 3 (1926), 105, and finally accepted by Harriet Monroe after a month's correspondence (published along with the poem) by *Poetry,* 29 (October 1926), 25. *White Buildings,* 1926. *American Poets: 1630–1930*, edited by Mark Van Doren. Boston: Little, Brown & Co., 1932. *Collected Poems,* 1933 and 1938. *Complete Poems,* 1958 and 1966.

First line: "Often beneath the wave, wide from this ledge"

B 9

"Ave Maria"

First published in *The American Caravan*, edited by Van Wyck Brooks, Lewis Mumford, Alfred Kreymborg, and Paul Rosenfeld. New York: Literary Guild of America, 1927. *The Bridge*, 1930, both editions. *Collected Poems*, 1933 and 1938. *Complete Poems*, 1958 and 1966.

First line: "Be with me, Luis de San Angel, now, —"

B 10

"Bacardi Spreads the Eagle's Wings"

First published as "Overheard" in *transition*, 9 (December 1927), 134. First published as "Bacardi Spreads the Eagle's Wings" in *Contempo*, 2 (July 5, 1932), 1, with two letters to the editor from Crane. *Collected Poems*, 1933 and 1938. *Complete Poems*, 1958 and 1966.

First line: "Pablo and Pedro and black Serafin"

B 11

"The Bathers"

First published in *The Pagan*, 2 (December 1917), 19. *Collected Poems*, 1933. *Complete Poems*, 1958 and 1966.

First line: "Two ivory women by a milky sea; —"

B 12

"Belle Isle"

Weber, *Hart Crane*, 1948. Philip Horton (in *Hart Crane: The Life of an American Poet*. New York: W. W. Norton, Inc.) claims that this became, in a much-altered form, "Voyages VI."

First line: "There was the river; —now there is"

B 13

"Black Tambourine"

Rejected by *The Dial;* first published in *The Double Dealer*, 1 (June 1921), 232. *White Buildings*, 1926. *Collected Poems*, 1933 and 1938. *Complete Poems*, 1958 and 1966.

First line: "The interests of a black man in a cellar"

B 14

"The Bridge of Estador"

Rejected by *The Dial;* first published in Weber, *Hart Crane*, 1948. *Complete Poems*, 1966.

First line: "Walk high on the bridge of Estador"

B 15
"The Broken Tower"
First published in *The New Republic*, 71 (June 8, 1932), 91. Crane thought he had submitted the poem to *Poetry*, but it was not received by either Harriet Monroe or Morton D. Zabel. *Collected Poems*, 1933 and 1938. *Complete Poems*, 1958 and 1966.

First line: "The bell-rope that gathers God at dawn"

B 16
"By Nilus Once I Knew . . ."
First published in *Poetry*, 41 (January 1933), 184, entitled "By Nilus Once." Published as "By Nilus Once I Knew . . ." in *Collected Poems*, 1933 and 1938. *Complete Poems*, 1958 and 1966.

First line: "Some old Egyptian joke is in the air"

B 17
"Cape Hatteras"
First published in *Saturday Review of Literature*, 6 (March 15, 1930), 821–822. *The Bridge*, 1930, both editions. *Collected Poems*, 1933 and 1938. *Complete Poems*, 1958 and 1966.

First line: "Imponderable the dinosaur"

B 18
"Carmen de Boheme"
First published in *Bruno's Bohemia*, 1 (March 1918), 2, as by "Harold H. Crane." Weber, *Hart Crane*, 1948. *Complete Poems*, 1966.

First line: "Sinuously winding through the room"

B 19
"Carrier Letter"
First published in *The Pagan*, 2–3 (April–May 1918), 20. *Collected Poems*, 1933. *Complete Poems*, 1958 and 1966.

First line: "My hands have not touched water since your hands, –"

B 20
"Chaplinesque"
Rejected by *The Dial, The New York Post Literary Review*, and *The Double Dealer;* first published in *Gargoyle*, 2 (December 1921), 24. *White Buildings*, 1926. *Collected Poems*, 1933

and 1938. *Complete Poems*, 1958. Charles Chaplin, *My Autobiography*. New York: Simon & Schuster, 1964. *Complete Poems*, 1966.

First line: "We make our meek adjustments"

B 21
"Children Dancing"
Weber, *Hart Crane*, 1948.

First line: "Where gables pack the rainless"

B 22
"The Circumstance"
First published in *Poetry*, 41 (January 1933), 179. *Collected Poems*, 1933 and 1938. *Complete Poems*, 1958.

First line: "The anointed stone, the corruscated crown"

B 23
"C 33"
First published in *Bruno's Weekly*, 3 (September 23, 1916), 1008, with the author's name printed incorrectly as "Harold H. Crone." Crane's first published poem, despite the assertions of Gorham Munson and Waldo Frank that Crane's first poem was published in *Bruno's Bohemia* when he was fifteen. Weber, *Hart Crane*, 1948. *Complete Poems*, 1966.

First line: "He has woven rose-vines"

C 33

HE has woven rose-vines
    About the empty heart of night,
And vented his long mellowed wines
Of dreaming on the desert white
With searing sophistry.
And he tented with far thruths he would form
The transient bosoms from the thorny tree.

O Materna! to enrich thy gold head
And wavering shoulders with a new light shed

From penitence, must needs bring pain,
And with it song of minor, broken strain.
But you who hear the lamp whisper thru night
Can trace paths tear-wet, and forget all blight.
                    HAROLD H. CRONE

"C 33," with Crane's name misspelled, from *Bruno's Weekly*
(B 23)

B 24
"Cutty Sark"
First published in *transition*, 3 (June 1927), 116–119. *Poetry*,
31 (October 1927), 27–30. *The Bridge*, 1930, both editions. *The
New Poetry*, edited by Harriet Monroe and Alice Corbin Henderson. New York: The Macmillan Company, 1932. *Collected Poems*,
1933 and 1938. *Complete Poems*, 1958 and 1966.

First line: "I met a man in South Street, tall–"

B 25
"The Dance"
First published in *The Dial*, 83 (October 1927), 329–332, under
the title "Powhatan's Daughter." Reprinted under that title in
An Anthology of Magazine Verse for 1928, edited by William
Stanley Braithwaite. New York: Harold Vinal, 1928. And again
in *Great Poems of the English Language*, edited by Wallace
Alvin Briggs. New York: Harlem Book Company, 1927. "Pow-
hatan's Daughter" was used later as the title of section 2 of *The
Bridge*. *The Bridge*, 1930, both editions. *Collected Poems*, 1933
and 1938. *Complete Poems*, 1958 and 1966.

First line: "The swift red flesh, a winter king–"

B 26
"East of Yucatan"
Not the title of a poem, but a title under which the following
poems were published in *transition*, 9 (December 1927), 131–
136: "Island Quarry," "Royal Palm," "Overheard," "El Idiota,"
and "The Hour."

B 27
"Echoes"
First published in *The Pagan*, 2 (October–November 1917), 39.
The first time he signed his work "Hart Crane" rather than
"Harold H. Crane." Weber, *Hart Crane*, 1948. *Seven Lyrics*,
1966. *Complete Poems*, 1966.

First line: "Slivers of rain upon the pane"

B 28
"Eldorado"
See "Indiana."

B 29
"El Idiota"
See "The Idiot."

B 30
"Enrich My Resignation"
First published in *Poetry*, 41 (January 1933), 186. *Literary Digest*, 115 (January 21, 1933), 38. *Collected Poems*, 1933 and 1938. *Complete Poems*, 1958.

First line: "Enrich my resignation as I usurp those far"

B 31
"Episode of Hands"
First published in Weber, *Hart Crane*, 1948, p. 384. *Complete Poems*, 1966.

First line: "The unexpected interest made him flush"

B 32
"Eternity"
First published in *The New Republic*, 74 (February 15, 1933), 15–16. *Collected Poems*, 1933 and 1938. *Complete Poems*, 1958 and 1966.

First line: "After it was over, though still gusting balefully"

B 33
"Euclid Avenue"
Weber, *Hart Crane*, 1948.

First line: "But so to be the denizen stingaree"

B 34
"Fear"
First published in *The Pagan*, 1–2 (April–May 1917), 11, as by "Harold H. Crane." *The Pagan Anthology*. New York: Pagan Publishing Company, [1918]. *Collected Poems*, 1933. *Complete Poems*, 1958 and 1966.

First line: "The host, he says that all is well"

B 35
"Forgetfulness"
First published in *The Pagan*, 3 (August–September 1918), 15. *A Second Pagan Anthology*. New York: Pagan Publishing Company, [1919]. *Collected Poems*, 1933. *Complete Poems*, 1958 and 1966.

First line: "Forgetfulness is like a song"

B 36
"For the Marriage of Faustus and Helen"

Part 2 of the poem appeared as "The Springs of Guilty Song" in *Broom*, 4 (January 1923), 131–132. Part 1 was rejected by *The Dial* under its new title. *Secession* (5 [September 1923], 1–4) printed a mutilated and incorrect version of "For the Marriage of Faustus and Helen," the second part being omitted entirely, as well as single lines here and there being dropped. The complete poem finally appeared in *Secession*, 7 (Winter 1924), 1–4. *White Buildings*, 1926. *Collected Poems*, 1933 and 1938. *Complete Poems*, 1958 and 1966.

First line: "The mind has shown itself at times"

B 37
"Garden Abstract"
Rejected by *The Fugitive, The New Republic,* and *The Dial;* first published in *The Little Review,* 7 (September–December 1920), 78. *White Buildings*, 1926. *Collected Poems*, 1933 and 1938. *Complete Poems*, 1958 and 1966.

First line: "The apple on its bough is her desire –"

B 38
"The Great Western Plains"
First published in *Gargoyle*, 3 (August 1922), 7. Weber, *Hart Crane,* 1948. *Complete Poems*, 1966.

First line: "The little voices of prairie dogs"

B 39
"The Harbor Dawn"
First published under the title "The Harbor Dawn: Brooklyn Heights," in *transition*, 3 (June 1927), 120–121. *The Bridge,* 1930, both editions. *An Anthology of the Younger Poets,* edited by Oliver Wells. Philadelphia: The Centaur Press, 1932. *Collected Poems,* 1933 and 1938. *Complete Poems,* 1958 and 1966.

First line in transition: "In sleep, – as though a shadow – bloomed aloud, – "

First line in The Bridge *(1930)*: "Insistently through sleep – a tide of voices – "

B 40
"Havana Rose"
First published in *Poetry*, 41 (January 1933), 180–182. *Collected Poems,* 1933 and 1938. *Complete Poems*, 1958 and 1966.

First line: "Let us strip the desk for action, now we have a house in"

B 41
"The Hive"
First published in *The Pagan*, 1 (March 1917), 36, as by "Harold Crane," *Collected Poems*, 1933. Horton, *Hart Crane*, 1937. *Complete Poems*, 1958 and 1966.

First line: "Up the chasm-walls of my bleeding heart"

B 42
"The Hour"
See "The Hurricane."

B 43
"The Hurricane"
First published as "The Hour" in *transition*, 9 (December 1927), 136. Published as "The Hurricane" in *The New Republic*, 67 (July 29, 1931), 277. *Collected Poems*, 1933. *Scholastic Magazine*, 26 (March 16, 1935), 11. *Collected Poems*, 1938. *Complete Poems*, 1958 and 1966.

First line: "Lo, Lord, Thou ridest"

B 44
"The Idiot"
First published under the title "El Idiota" in *transition*, 9 (December 1927), 135. Published as "The Idiot" in *Collected Poems*, 1933 and 1938. *Complete Poems*, 1958 and 1966.

First line: "Sheer over to the other side, – for see –"

B 45
"Imperator Victus"
First published in *Poetry*, 41 (January 1933), 180. *Collected Poems*, 1933 and 1938. *Complete Poems*, 1958 and 1966.

First line: "Big guns again"

B 46
"In a Court"
First published in *Literary America*, 1 (September 1934), 14. Includes four letters to Samuel Loveman. Weber, *Hart Crane*, 1948.

First line: "His hand changed in the kitchen"

B 47
"Indiana"
First published as "Eldorado" in *Poetry,* 36 (April 1930), 13–15.
Published as "Indiana" in *The Bridge,* 1930, both editions. *Collected Poems,* 1933 and 1938. *Complete Poems,* 1958 and 1966.

First line: "The morning glory, climbing the morning long"

B 48
"In Shadow"
First published in *The Little Review,* 4 (December 1917), 50.
White Buildings, 1926. *Collected Poems,* 1933 and 1938. *"The
Little Review" Anthology,* edited by Margaret Anderson. New
York: Hermitage House, 1953. *Complete Poems,* 1958 and 1966.
In November 1918 Crane tried to get this poem and five other
poems, which had previously appeared in *The Pagan,* published
by Rev. Charles C. Bubb at the Church Head Press, Cleveland, as
a modest pamphlet, tentatively entitled "Six Lyrics."

First line: "Out in the late amber afternoon"

B 49
"Interior"
First published in *The Modernist,* 3 (November 1919), 28.
Weber, *Hart Crane,* 1948. *Complete Poems,* 1966.

First line: "It sheds a shy solemnity"

B 50
"Interludium"
First published in 1924, 1 (July 1924), 2. Weber, *Hart Crane,*
1948, prints two versions. *Gaston Lachaise.* Los Angeles: Los
Angeles County Museum of Art, 1963, back inside cover. A catalogue of an exhibition of the work of Lachaise. The poem's subtitle is "To 'La Montagne,' by Lachaise." *Complete Poems,* 1966.

First line: "Thy time is thee to wend"

B 51
"Island Quarry"
First published in *transition,* 9 (December 1927), 132. *Collected Poems,* 1933 and 1938. Complete Poems, 1958 and 1966.

First line: "Square sheets—they saw the marble only into"

B 52
"Lachrymae Christi"

First published in *The Fugitive*, 4 (December 1925), 102–103. *White Buildings*, 1926. *Collected Poems*, 1933 and 1938. *Complete Poems*, 1958 and 1966.

First line: "Whitely, while benzine"

B 53

"Legend"

First published in *The Fugitive*, 4 (September 1925), 77. *White Buildings*, 1926. *American Poets: 1630–1930*, edited by Mark Van Doran. Boston: Little, Brown & Co., 1932. *Collected Poems*, 1933 and 1938. *Complete Poems*, 1958 and 1966.

First line: "As silent as a mirror is believed"

B 54

"Legende"

First published in *The Modernist*, 3 (November 1919), 28. Weber, *Hart Crane*, 1948. *Complete Poems*, 1966. "Legend" and "Legende" are two different poems.

First line: "The tossing loneliness of many nights"

B 55

"Lenses"

Weber, *Hart Crane*, 1948. *Complete Poems*, 1966. Weber reports that the typescript of the poem indicates that it was originally intended for *The Bridge*: "directly preceding 'Tunnel'/VII or Viii/Lenses."

First line: "In the focus of the evening there is this island with"

B 56

"Locutions Des Pierrots"

Three translations from Jules Laforgue, first published in *The Double Dealer*, 3 (May 1922), 261–262. Weber, *Hart Crane*, 1948, pp. 388–389. *Sewanee Review*, 58 (July–September 1950), 442–444. *Complete Poems*, 1966.

First line: "Your eyes, those pools with soft rushes"

B 57

"The Mango Tree"

First published in *transition*, 18 (November 1929), 95. *Collected Poems*, 1933 and 1938. *Complete Poems*, 1958 and 1966.

First line: "Let them return, saying you blush again for the Great Great-Grand —"

B 58
"March"
First published in *larus: The Celestial Visitor*, 1 (March 1927), 14. *Collected Poems*, 1933 and 1938. *Complete Poems*, 1958 and 1966.

First line: "Awake to the cold light"

B 59
"The Masters"
Weber, *Hart Crane*, 1948.

First line: "Their brains are smooth machines that colonize"

B 60
"The Mermen"
First published in *The Dial*, 85 (September 1928), 230, incorrectly listed by Weber in *Complete Poems*, 1966, as July 1928. *An Anthology of Magazine Verse for 1929*, edited by William Stanley Braithwaite. New York: George Scully and Co., 1929. *Collected Poems*, 1933 and 1938. *Complete Poems*, 1958 and 1966.

First line: "Buddhas and the engines serve us underseas"

B 61
"Mirror of Narcissus"
Weber, *Hart Crane*, 1948.

First line: "They judge, whose strictures of their sight"

B 62
"Modern Craft"
First published in *The Pagan*, 2 (January 1918), 37. *Collected Poems*, 1933. *Complete Poems*, 1958 and 1966.

First line: "Though I have touched her flesh of moons"

B 63
"Moment Fugue"
First published in *transition*, 15 (February 1929), 102. *Collected Poems*, 1933 and 1938. *Complete Poems*, 1958 and 1966.

First line: "The syphilitic selling violets calmly"

B 64
"The Moth that God Made Blind"
First published in *Columbia Library Columns,* 10 (November 1960), 24–26. *Complete Poems,* 1966.

First line: "Among cocoa-nut palms of a far oasis"

B 65
"My Grandmother's Love Letters"
Rejected by *The Little Review;* first published in *The Dial,* 68 (April 1920), 457, the first poem for which he was paid (ten dollars). *White Buildings,* 1926. *American Poets: 1630–1930,* edited by Mark Van Doren. Boston: Little, Brown & Co., 1932. *Collected Poems,* 1933 and 1938. *Complete Poems,* 1958 and 1966.

First line: "There are no stars to-night"

B 66
"A Name for All"
First published in *The Dial,* 86 (April 1929), 297. *An Anthology of Magazine Verse for 1929,* edited by William Stanley Braithwaite. New York: George Scully and Co., 1929, p. 74–75. *Collected Poems,* 1933 and 1938. *Complete Poems,* 1958 and 1966.

First line: "Moonmoth and grasshopper that flee our page"

B 67
"National Winter Garden"
First published in *The Calendar* (London), 4 (April–July 1927), 109. *The Bridge,* 1930, both editions. *Collected Poems,* 1933 and 1938. *Complete Poems,* 1958 and 1966.

First line: "Outspoken buttocks in pink beads"

B 68
"North Labrador"
Rejected by *The Little Review;* first published in *The Modernist,* 3 (November 1919), 28. *White Buildings,* 1926. *Collected Poems,* 1933 and 1938. *Complete Poems,* 1958 and 1966.

First line: "A land of leaning ice"

B 69
"O Carib Isle!"
First published in *transition,* 1 (April 1927), 101–102. *Poetry* 31 (October 1927), 30–31. *Collected Poems,* 1933 and 1938. *Complete Poems,* 1958 and 1966.

First line: "The tarantula rattling at the lily's foot"

B 70
"October–November"
First published in *The Pagan*, 1 (November–December 1916), 33, as by "Harold H. Crane." *The Pagan Anthology.* New York: Pagan Publishing Company, [1918]. *Collected Poems*, 1933. *Complete Poems*, 1958 and 1966.

First line: "Indian-summer-sun"

B 71
"Of an Evening Pulling Off a Little Experience (with the english language)"
Susan Jenkins Brown, *Robber Rocks: Letters and Memories of Hart Crane, 1923–1932.* Middletown, Connecticut: Wesleyan University Press, 1969.

First line: "Wrists web rythms"

B 72
"Old Song"
First published in *The New Republic*, 51 (August 10, 1927), 309. *Collected Poems*, 1933 and 1938. *Complete Poems*, 1958 and 1966.

First line: "Thy absence overflows the rose –"

B 73
"Overheard"
See "Bacardi Spreads the Eagle's Wings."

B 74
"Oyster"
Weber, *Hart Crane*, 1948.

First line: "Time is not to be worn, strapped to the wrist"

B 75
"Paraphrase"
First published in *The Fugitive*, 4 (September 1925), 78. *White Buildings*, 1926. *American Poets: 1630–1930*, edited by Mark Van Doren. Boston: Little, Brown & Co., 1932. *Collected Poems*, 1933 and 1938. *Complete Poems*, 1958 and 1966.

First line: "Of a steady winking beat between"

B 76
"Passage"
Rejected by *The Dial* and *The Criterion;* first published in *The Calendar* (London), 3 (1926), 106–107. *White Buildings,* 1926. *Collected Poems,* 1933 and 1938. *Complete Poems,* 1958 and 1966.

First line: "Where the cedar leaf divides the sky"

B 77
"Pastorale"
First published in *The Dial,* 71 (October 1921), 422. *White Buildings,* 1926. *Collected Poems,* 1933 and 1938. *Complete Poems,* 1958 and 1966.

First line: "No more violets"

B 78
"A Persuasion"
First published in *The Measure,* 8 (October 1921), 14. Weber, *Hart Crane,* 1948. *Complete Poems,* 1966.

First line: "If she waits late at night"

B 79
"Phantom Bark"
First published in *Poetry,* 41 (January 1933), 185. *Literary Digest,* 115 (January 21, 1933), 38. *Collected Poems,* 1933 and 1938. *Complete Poems,* 1958 and 1966.

First line: "So dream thy sails, O phantom bark"

B 80
"The Pillar and the Post"
Weber, *Hart Crane,* 1948.

First line: "What you may yank up readiest, Yank –"

B 81
"A Placement"
Weber, *Hart Crane,* 1948.

First line: "Shall I subsume the shadow of the world"

B 82
"Porphyro in Akron"
Rejected by *The Dial* and *The Little Review;* first published in

The Double Dealer, 2 (August–September 1921), 53. Weber, *Hart Crane*, 1948. *Complete Poems*, 1966.

First line: "Greeting the dawn"

B 83
"Possessions"
First published in *The Little Review*, 10 (Spring 1924), 18–19. *White Buildings*, 1926. *Collected Poems*, 1933 and 1938. *Complete Poems*, 1966.

First line: "Witness now this trust! the rain"

B 84
"Poster"
See "Voyages I."

B 85
"Postscript"
First published in *The Pagan*, 2–3 (April–May 1918), 20. *Collected Poems*, 1933. *Complete Poems*, 1958 and 1966.

First line: "Though now but marble are the marble urns"

B 86
"A Postscript"
First published in *Poetry*, 41 (January 1933), 185–186. *Literary Digest*, 115 (January 21, 1933), 38. *Collected Poems*, 1933 and 1938. *Complete Poems*, 1958 and 1966. "Postscript" and "A Postscript" are two different poems.

First line: "Friendship agony! words came to me"

B 87
"Powhatan's Daughter"
See "The Dance."

B 88
"Praise for an Urn"
First published in *The Dial*, 72 (June 1922), 606. *An Anthology of Magazine Verse for 1922*, edited by William Stanley Braithwaite. Boston: Small, Maynard, 1923, p. 57. *The Calendar* (London), 3 (1926), 108. *White Buildings*, 1926. *An Anthology of the Younger Poets*, edited by Oliver Wells. Philadelphia: The Centaur Press, 1932. *American Poets: 1630–1930*, edited by Mark Van Doren. Boston: Little, Brown & Co., 1932. *Collected Poems*, 1933 and 1938. *Complete Poems*, 1958 and 1966.

First line: "It was a kind and northern face"

B 89
"Purgatorio"
First published in *Poetry*, 41 (January 1933), 178. *Collected Poems*, 1933 and 1938. *Complete Poems*, 1958 and 1966.

First line: "My country, O my land, my friends –"

B 90
"Recitative"
First published in *The Little Review*, 10 (Spring 1924), 19. *White Buildings*, 1926. *Collected Poems*, 1933 and 1938. *Complete Poems*, 1958 and 1966.

First line: "Regard the capture here, O Janus-faced –"

B 91
"Reliquary"
First published in *Poetry*, 41 (January 1933), 77. *Collected Poems*, 1933 and 1938. *Complete Poems*, 1958 and 1966.

First line: "Tenderness and resolution"

B 92
"Reply"
First published in *Poetry*, 41 (January 1933), 183–184. *Collected Poems*, 1933 and 1938. *Complete Poems*, 1958 and 1966.

First line: "Thou canst read nothing except through appetite"

B 93
"Repose of Rivers"
First published in *The Dial*, 81 (September 1926), 204. *White Buildings*, 1926. *The New Poetry*, edited by Harriet Monroe and Alice Corbin Henderson. New York: The Macmillan Company, 1932. *American Poets: 1630–1930*, edited by Mark Van Doren. Boston: Little, Brown & Co., 1932. *Collected Poems*, 1933 and 1938. *Complete Poems*, 1958 and 1966.

First line: "The willows carried a slow sound"

B 94
"The Return"
First published in *The New Republic*, 74 (February 15, 1933), 16. *Collected Poems*, 1933 and 1938. *Complete Poems*, 1958.

First line: "The sea raised up a campanile . . . The wind I heard"

B 95
"The River"
Rejected by *The Little Review;* first published in *The Second American Caravan,* edited by Alfred Kreymborg, Lewis Mumford, and Paul Rosenfeld. New York: The Macauley Company, 1928, pp. 113–117. *The Bridge,* 1930, both editions. *Collected Poems,* 1933 and 1938. Complete Poems, 1958 and 1966.

First line: "Stick your patent name on a signboard"

B 96
"Royal Palm"
First published in *transition,* 9 (December 1927), 133. *Modern American Poetry and Modern British Poetry,* edited by Louis Untermeyer. New York: Harcourt, Brace and Company, 1930. *Collected Poems,* 1933 and 1938. *Complete Poems,* 1958 and 1966.

First line: "Green rustlings, more-than-regal charities"

B 97
"The Sad Indian"
First published in *Poetry,* 41 (January 1933), 182. *Collected Poems,* 1933 and 1938. *Complete Poems,* 1958 and 1966.

First line: "Sad heart, the gymnast of inertia, does not count"

B 98
"A Song for Happy Feast Days"
American Weave, 30 (December 1966), 1. A quatrain inscribed on a preliminary leaf of *The Complete Poetical Works of Robert Burns* (New York: Thomas H. Crowell & Co.), signed "To Aunt Alice | from Harold Crane | Xmas of 1914." The Burns volume is owned by Loring Williams, South Berwick, Maine. See Joseph Katz, "CALM Addendum No. 1: Hart Crane," *Papers of the Bibliographical Society of America,* 63 (2nd Quarter 1969), 130.

First line: "A song for happy feast days"

B 99
"Sonnet"
Weber, *Hart Crane,* 1948.

First line: "What miles I gather up unto you"

B 100
"Southern Cross"
First published in *The Calendar* (London), 4 (April–July 1927),
107–108. *The Bridge*, 1930, both editions. *An Anthology of the
Younger Poets*, edited by Oliver Wells. Philadelphia: The Cen-
taur Press, 1932. *Collected Poems*, 1933 and 1938. *Complete
Poems*, 1958 and 1966.

First line: "I wanted you, nameless Woman of the South"

B 101
"The Springs of Guilty Song"
See "For the Marriage of Faustus and Helen."

B 102
"Stark Major"
Rejected by *The Dial;* first published in *The Fugitive*, 2 (August
1923), 120, with the notation that it "qualified for the Nashville
Prize." *White Buildings*, 1926. *Collected Poems*, 1933 and
1938. *Complete Poems*, 1958 and 1966.

First line: "The lover's death, how regular"

B 103
"Three Songs from *The Bridge*"
A general title for "Southern Cross," "National Winter Garden,"
and "Virginia," in *The Calendar* (London), 4 (April–July 1927),
107–110. The title "Three Songs" is used in *The Bridge*, 1930,
both editions. *Collected Poems*, 1933 and 1938. *Complete Poems*,
1958 and 1966.

B 104
"To Brooklyn Bridge"
First published in *The Dial*, 82 (June 1927), 489–490. *Poetry*,
37 (November 1930), 108–109. "From Mr. Crane's book, *The
Bridge*, we reprint the invocation, as more representative than
the section in *Poetry* last April." Crane had been awarded the
Helen Haire Levinson Prize of $200 for *The Bridge*. *The Bridge*,
1930, both editions. *The New Poetry*, edited by Harriet Monroe
and Alice Corbin Henderson. New York: The Macmillan Com-
pany, 1932. *American Poets: 1630–1930*, edited by Mark Van
Doren. Boston: Little, Brown & Co., 1932. *Collected Poems*, 1933
and 1938. *Complete Poems*, 1958. *A Dial Miscellany*, edited by
William Wasserstrom. Syracuse, New York: Syracuse University
Press, 1963. *Complete Poems*, 1958 and 1966.

First line: "How many dawns, chill from his rippling rest"

B 105
"To Emily Dickinson"
First published in *The Nation*, 124 (June 29, 1927), 718. *An Anthology of Magazine Verse for 1927*, edited by William Stanley Braithwaite. Boston: B. J. Brimmer, 1927. *Collected Poems*, 1933 and 1938. *Complete Poems*, 1958 and 1966.

First line: "You who desired so much – in vain to ask –"

B 106
"To Liberty"
First published in Weber, *Hart Crane*, 1948. *Complete Poems*, 1966.

First line: "Out of the seagull cries and wind"

B 107
"To Portapovitch"
First published as "To Potapovitch" in *The Modern School*, 6 (March 1919), 80. *Collected Poems*, 1933. *Complete Poems*, 1958. Published as "To Portapovitch" in *Complete Poems*, 1966.

First line: "Vault on the opal carpet of the sun"

B 108
"To Shakespeare"
First published in *The New Republic*, 74 (April 5, 1933), 212. *Collected Poems*, 1933 and 1938. *Complete Poems*, 1958. *Etudes Anglaises*, 17 (October–December 1964), 586. *Complete Poems*, 1966. Another version of this poem, "The Tree: Great William," was published as a footnote to "To Shakespeare" in *Collected Poems*, 1933, and *Complete Poems*, 1958. It appears as a separate poem in *Collected Poems*, 1938.

First line: "Through torrid entrances pass icy poles"

B 109
"To the Cloud Juggler"
First published in *transition*, 19–20 (June 1930), 223. *Collected Poems*, 1933 and 1938. *Complete Poems*, 1958 and 1966.

First line: "What you may cluster 'round the knees of space"

B 110
"To the Empress Josephine's Statue"

First published in Weber, *Hart Crane*, 1948. *Complete Poems*, 1966.

First line: "You who contain, augmented tears, explosions"

B 111
"A Traveler Born"
First published in *The New Republic*, 74 (February 15, 1933), 16. *Collected Poems*, 1933 and 1938. *Complete Poems*, 1958.

First line: "Of sailors – those two Corsicans at Marseille"

B 112
"The Tunnel"
First published in *The Criterion*, 6 (November 1927), 398–402. *Twentieth Century Poetry*, edited by John Drinkwater, Henry Seidel Canby, and William Rose Benét. Cambridge, Massachusetts: Houghton Mifflin Company, 1929. *Modern American Poetry and Modern British Poetry*, edited by Louis Untermeyer. New York: Harcourt, Brace and Company, 1930. *The Bridge*, 1930, both editions. *Collected Poems*, 1933 and 1938. *Complete Poems*, 1958 and 1966.

First line: "Performances, assortments, résumés – "

B 113
[Untitled]
John Unterecker, *Voyager: A Life of Hart Crane*. New York: Farrar, Straus & Giroux, 1969, p. 326.

First line: "This way where November takes the leaf"

B 114
"The Urn"
Not the title of a poem but a general title used in *Poetry*, 41 (January 1933), 177–186, for the following poems: "Reliquary," "Purgatorio," "The Circumstance," "Imperator Victus," "Havana Rose," "The Sad Indian," "The Visible the Untrue," "Reply," "By Nilus Once," "Phantom Bark," "A Postscript," and "Enrich My Resignation."

B 115
"Van Winkle"
Rejected by *The New Republic;* first published in *transition*, 7 (October 1927), 128–129. *The Bridge*, 1930, both editions. *Modern American Poetry and Modern British Poetry*, edited by Louis Untermeyer. New York: Harcourt, Brace and Company, 1930. *Collected Poems*, 1958 and 1966.

First line: "Macadam, gun-grey as the tunny's belt"

B 116
"Virginia"
First published in *The Calendar* (London), 4 (April–July 1927), 110. *The Bridge,* 1930, both editions. *Collected Poems,* 1933 and 1938. *Complete Poems,* 1958 and 1966.

First line: "O rain at seven"

B 117
"The Visible the Untrue"
First published in *Poetry,* 41 (January 1933), 182–183. *Collected Poems,* 1933 and 1938. *Complete Poems,* 1958 and 1966.

First line: "Yes, I being"

B 118
"Voyages"
A general title used for "Voyages II," "Voyages III," "Voyages V," and "Voyages VI," in *The Little Review,* 12 (Spring 1926), 13–14. These four "Voyages" had been accepted by *The Guardian,* and Allen Tate had decided to write a short essay on them for a future issue. The October 1925 issue was the last to appear, however, and the poems, announced for the next issue, were not printed. "Voyages" is also the title used for "Voyages I, II, III, IV, V, VI," in *White Buildings,* 1926. *Collected Poems,* 1933 and 1938. *Voyages,* The Museum of Modern Art, 1957. *Complete Poems,* 1958 and 1966.

B 119
"Voyages I"
Rejected by *The Dial* and *The Little Review;* first published as "Poster" in *Secession,* 4 (January 1923), 20. Appeared as "Voyages I" in *White Buildings,* 1926. *Collected Poems,* 1933 and 1938. *Voyages,* The Museum of Modern Art, 1957. *Complete Poems,* 1958 and 1966.

First line: "Above the fresh ruffles of the surf"

B 120
"Voyages II"
First published as "Voyages I" in *The Little Review,* 12 (Spring 1926), 13–14. Appeared as "Voyages II" in *White Buildings,* 1926. *Modern American Poetry and Modern British Poetry,* edited by Louis Untermeyer. New York: Harcourt, Brace and

Company, 1930. *The New Poetry,* edited by Harriet Monroe and Alice Corbin Henderson. New York: The Macmillan Company, 1932. *The Book of Living Verse,* edited by Louis Untermeyer. New York: Harcourt, Brace and Company, 1932. *An Anthology of the Younger Poets,* edited by Oliver Wells. Philadelphia: The Centaur Press, 1932. *Collected Poems,* 1933 and 1938. *Voyages,* The Museum of Modern Art, 1957. *Complete Poems,* 1958 and 1966.

First line: "—And yet this great wink of eternity"

B 121
"Voyages III"
First published as "Voyages II" in *The Little Review,* 12 (Spring 1926), 14. Appeared as "Voyages III" in *White Buildings,* 1926. *Collected Poems,* 1933 and 1938. *Voyages,* The Museum of Modern Art, 1957. *Complete Poems,* 1958 and 1966.

First line: "Infinite consanguinity it bears"

B 122
"Voyages V"
First published as "Voyages III" in *The Little Review,* 12 (Spring 1926), 14. Appeared as "Voyages V" in *White Buildings,* 1926. *An Anthology of the Younger Poets,* edited by Oliver Wells. Philadelphia: The Centaur Press, 1932. *Collected Poems,* 1933 and 1938. *Inventario,* 1 (Fall–Winter 1946–1947), 98. *Voyages,* The Museum of Modern Art, 1957. *Complete Poems,* 1958 and 1966.

First line: "Meticulous, past midnight in clear rime"

B 123
"Voyages VI"
First published as "Voyages IV" in *The Little Review,* 12 (Spring 1926), 15. Appeared as "Voyages VI" in *White Buildings,* 1926. *The Third Book of Modern Verse,* edited by Jessie B. Rittenhouse. New York: Houghton Mifflin Company, 1927. *Modern American Poetry and Modern British Poetry,* edited by Louis Untermeyer. New York: Harcourt, Brace and Company, 1930. *Collected Poems,* 1933 and 1938. *Inventario,* 1 (Fall–Winter 1946–1947), 99. *Voyages,* The Museum of Modern Art, 1957. *Complete Poems,* 1958 and 1966.

First line: "Where icy and bright dungeons lift"

B 124
"The Wine Menagerie"

Rejected by *The Criterion;* first published in *The Dial,* 80 (May 1926), 370, under the title "Again" and significantly altered by the editor, Marianne Moore. Appeared in this altered form under the title "Again" in *An Anthology of Magazine Verse for 1926,* edited by William Stanley Braithwaite. Boston: B. J. Brimmer Co., 1926. First published as "The Wine Menagerie" without Miss Moore's alterations in *White Buildings,* 1926. *Collected Poems,* 1933 and 1938. *Complete Poems,* 1958 and 1966.

First line as "Again": "What in this heap in which the serpent pries"

First line as "The Wine Menagerie": "Invariably when wine redeems the sight"

B 125
"With a Photograph to Zell, Now Bound for Spain"
First published as a broadside. Cambridge, Massachusetts: Ibex Press, 1966. *Columbia Library Columns,* 15 (May 1966), 2. *Forum,* 5 (Summer 1967), 42.

First line: "From Brooklyn Heights one sees the bay"

PROSE

B 126
"The Case Against Nietzsche"
First published in *The Pagan,* 2–3 (April–May 1918), 34–35. *Twice a Year,* 12–13 (1945), 426–427. Brom Weber, *Hart Crane.* New York: The Bodley Press, 1948. *Complete Poems,* 1966.

B 127
"Critical Fragment"
Weber, *Hart Crane,* 1948.

B 128
"Editorial Note to a Patriotic Poem"
The Pagan, 2–3 (April–May 1918), 28. Informs the readers that the editors had some reservations in publishing a patriotic poem.

B 129
"Eight More Harvard Poets"
First published in *S4N,* 4 (March–April 1923), unpaged. *Twice a Year,* 12–13 (1945), 438–439. Weber, *Hart Crane,* 1948. *Complete Poems,* 1966.

B 130
"From Haunts of Proserpine"
First published in *Poetry,* 40 (April 1932), 44-47. *Twice a Year,*
12-13 (1945), 446-449. Weber, *Hart Crane,* 1948. *Complete
Poems,* 1966. A review of James Whaler's "Green River: A Poem
for Rafinesque."

B 131
"General Aims and Theories"
First published in Philip Horton, *Hart Crane: The Life of an
American Poet.* New York: W. W. Norton & Co., 1937. Complete
Poems, 1966.

B 132
"The Ghetto and Other Poems by Lola Ridge"
First published in *The Pagan,* 3 (January 1919), 55-56. *Twice
a Year,* 12-13 (1945), 428-430. Weber, *Hart Crane,* 1948.

B 133
"Joyce and Ethics"
First published in *The Little Review,* 5 (July 1918), 65. *Twice
a Year,* 12-13 (1945), 427-428. Weber, *Hart Crane,* 1948. *"The
Little Review" Anthology,* edited by Margaret Anderson. New
York: Hermitage House, 1953. *Complete Poems,* 1966. *James
Joyce: The Cultural Heritage,* edited by Robert H. Deming.
London: Routledge & Kegan Paul, 1970.

B 134
"The Last Chord"
The Pagan, 2-3 (April–May 1918), 55-56. A brief review of
theater in the Village: Eugene O'Neill's *Ile,* Edna St. Vincent
Millay's *Two Slatterns and a King,* and Alfred Kreymborg's
Maniken and Miniken.

B 135
"Minna and Myself"
First published in *The Pagan,* 3 (February 1919), 59-60. *Twice
a Year,* 12-13 (1945), 430-431. Weber, *Hart Crane,* 1948. *Complete Poems,* 1966. A review of Maxwell Bodenheim's *Minna
and Myself.*

B 136
"Modern Poetry"
First published in *Revolt in the Arts: A Survey of the Creation,
Distribution, and Appreciation of Art in America,* edited by

Oliver M. Sayler. New York: Brentano's, 1930, pp. 294–298. *Collected Poems,* 1933. *Twice a Year,* 12–13 (1945), 449–452. *Complete Poems,* 1958 and 1966.

B 137
"A Note on Minns"
First published in *The Little Review,* 7 (September–December 1920), 60. *Twice a Year,* 12–13 (1945), 433. Weber, *Hart Crane,* 1948. *Complete Poems,* 1966.

B 138
"Proclamation"
transition, 16–17 (June 1929), 13. A manifesto of twelve assertions which are responses to the opening generalization: "Tired of the spectacle of short stories, novels, poems and plays still written on naturalism, and desirous of crystallizing a viewpoint . . . we hereby declare that: . . . " It is doubtful that Crane wrote any part of the proclamation, but he did sign it along with Kay Boyle, Whitt Burnett, Caresse Crosby, Harry Crosby, Martha Foley, Stuart Gilbert, A. L. Gillespie, Leigh Hoffman, Eugene Jolas, Elliot Paul, Douglas Rigby, Theo Rutra, Robert Sage, Harold J. Salemson, and Laurence Vail. Horton claims that Crane was sorry he signed it.

B 139
"Sherwood Anderson"
First published in *The Double Dealer,* 2 (July 1921), 42–45. *Twice a Year,* 12–13 (1945), 433–438. Weber, *Hart Crane,* 1948. *Complete Poems,* 1966. A review of Sherwood Anderson's *Poor White.*

B 140
"Sherwood Anderson"
First published in *The Pagan,* 4 (September 1919), 60–61. *Twice a Year,* 12–13 (1945), 431–433. Weber, *Hart Crane,* 1948. *Complete Poems,* 1966. A review of Sherwood Anderson's *Winesburg, Ohio.*

LETTERS

B 141
To William Slater Brown
Phrases, sentences, and paragraphs from previously unpublished letters are included in John Unterecker, *Voyager: A Life*

of Hart Crane. New York: Farrar, Straus, & Giroux, 1969. The page number of *Voyager* is in parentheses following the date of each letter: October 11, 1925 (401); December 16 (?), 1928 (575–576); November 11, 1929 (606); April 6, 1931 (652).

B 142

To William Slater Brown and Susan Jenkins Brown

"Hart Crane: The End of the Harvest," *The Southern Review*, 4 (Autumn 1968), 945–1014. Eleven of the twenty-one letters were previously published: no. 5 (216), no. 6 (242), no. 7 (245), no. 9 (273), no. 12 (292), no. 13 (294), no. 14 (298), no. 15 (300), no. 16 (303), no. 18 (323), and no. 21 (373). (The numbers in parentheses refer to those in *The Letters of Hart Crane 1916–1932*. The texts are taken from full original letters or full verbatim typescripts. The letters previously published in Weber are published here in full, with the names of the persons referred to (with an exception) used in full instead of initials except where Crane himself used initials as a shortcut. Edited with an introduction and reminiscences by Susan Jenkins Brown. These letters also appear in Susan Jenkins Brown, *Robber Rocks: Letters and Memories of Hart Crane, 1923–1932*. Middletown, Connecticut: Wesleyan University Press, 1969.

B 143

To William Slater Brown and Susan Jenkins Brown

A portion of the letter of July 28, 1925, previously unpublished, appears in Unterecker, *Voyager*, 1969, p. 396.

B 144

To George Bryan

Four letters from Crane to George Bryan, *The Free Lance*, 8, no. 1 (1963), 3–7. These letters are numbered VIII, XVII, XX, and XXI in *Twenty-one Letters from Hart Crane to George Bryan*, 1968.

B 145

To Harry Candee

A portion of the letter dated February 26, 1922, previously unpublished, appears in Unterecker, *Voyager*, 1969, p. 239.

B 146

To *Contempo*

Contempo, 2 (July 5, 1932), 1. Two letters dated March 11, 1932, and April 20, 1932 (*The Letters*, no. 403).

B 147
To Malcolm Cowley
Previously unpublished letters appear in Susan Jenkins Brown, *Robber Rocks: Letters and Memories of Hart Crane, 1923–1932.* Middletown, Connecticut: Wesleyan University Press, 1969. December 10, 1923; March 27, 1928 (to MC and Peggy Baird Cowley); August 1928; October 24, 1928; August 22, 1929; February 18, 1932 (to MC and Muriel Cowley). Portions of the letters of December 10, 1923, and August 1928 also appear in Unterecker, *Voyager,* 1969. The following letters to Cowley published in part in *The Letters,* 1952, are therein published in full: 225, 237, 295, 311, 319, 328, 362, 371, 384.

B 148
To Peggy Baird Cowley
Phrases, sentences, and paragraphs from previously unpublished letters are included in Unterecker, *Voyager,* 1969. The page number of *Voyager* is in parentheses following the date of each letter: Between September 15 and November 15, 1931 (696); November 20, 1931 (702); January 12, 1932 (718 and 720); January 31, 1932 (723).

B 149
To Bess Crane
Phrases, sentences, and paragraphs from previously unpublished letters are included in Unterecker, *Voyager,* 1969. The page number of *Voyager* is in parentheses following the date of each letter: September 18, 1931 (690, 692, and 693); October 4, 1931 (685 and 696); October 20, 1931 (686); November 5, 1931 (698); January 7, 1932 (717); January 9, 1932 (713 and 716); March 8, 1932 (733 and 734); March 15, 1932 (736).

B 150
To Clarence A. Crane
Alan Trachtenberg, *Brooklyn Bridge: Fact and Symbol* (New York: Oxford University Press, 1965), p. 157, contains a portion of Crane's letter to his father dated June 21, 1927. "Time and space is the myth of the modern world and it is interesting to see how any victory in the field is heralded by the mass of humanity. In a way my Bridge is a manifestation of the same general subject. Maybe I'm just a little jealous of Lindy [Charles Lindbergh]!"

B 151
To Clarence A. Crane
Phrases, sentences, and paragraphs from previously unpub-

lished letters are included in Unterecker, *Voyager*, 1969. The page number of *Voyager* is in parentheses following the date of each letter: May 20, 1926 (439 and 441); September 2, 1926 (453); October 31, 1926 (458); November 10, 1926 (460); April 23, 1927 (489); May 24, 1927 (496); May 24, 1927 (496); June 21, 1927 (506); November 10, 1927 (515 and 517); June 14.

B 152
To Grace Hart Crane
Phrases, sentences, and paragraphs from previously unpublished letters are included in Unterecker, *Voyager*, 1969. The page number of *Voyager* is in parentheses following the date of each letter: November 5, 1910 (24); January 2, 1917 (55); January 5, 1917 (53 and 59); February 1, 1917 (60); March 23, 1917 (69); April 3, 1917 (71); October 5, 1917 (90 and 108); October 8, 1917 (91); October 9, 1917 (109); October 26, 1917 (96); February 23, 1919 (126 and 137); February 27, 1919 (125 and 133); March 21, 1919 (128, 129, 133, and 137); March 29, 1919 (125 and 138); April 12, 1919 (129 and 133); April 20, 1919 (126, 131, and 137); May 3, 1919 (131 and 137); September 22, 1919 (146); October 7, 1922 (263); October 31, 1919 (144 and 147); June 18, 1923 (303, 307, and 311); July 2, 1923 (300); July 14, 1923 (303); September 21, 1923 (311); October 24, 1923 (321); October 26, 1923 (322); November 21, 1923 (337); November 27, 1923 (330 and 334); December 10, 1923 (337); December 14, 1923 (330); January 4, 1924 (342); January 9, 1924 (344); January 12, 1924 (345); January 18, 1924 (349); January 29, 1924 (362); February 15, 1924 (353); February 23, 1924 (350); February 26, 1924 (351); April 3, 1924 (353); April 3, 1924 (354); April 3, 1924 (354); April 20, 1924 (355); April 20, 1924 (356); May 4, 1924 (360); July 4, 1924 (369); September 4, 1924 (366); October 14, 1924 (364); January 29, 1925 (384); February 10, 1925 (373); July 19, 1925 (387); July 20, 1925 (392); October 24, 1925 (410); January 27, 1926 (419); April 24, 1926 (434 and 436); May 3, 1926 (437); May 8, 1926 (437, 439, and 441); August 28, 1926 (452); September 6, 1926 (455); January 17, 1927 (470); January 27, 1927 (470); March 1, 1927 (484); March 12, 1927 (484); March 28, 1927 (479); April 28, 1927 (490); April 30, 1927 (491); May 9, 1927 (493 and 495); May 9, 1927 (498); June 4, 1927 (498); June 14, 1927 (497); June 18, 1927 (505); July 4, 1927 (505); July 8, 1927 (499 and 505); November 3, 1927 (516 and 517); June 21, 1928 (545). The following letters are published in whole or part in Thomas S. W. Lewis, "Hart Crane and His Mother: A Correspondence," *Salmagundi*, 9 (Spring 1969), 61–87: January 5, 1917; October 8, 1917; February 24, 1919; March 29, 1919; April 2, 1919;

Easter, 1919; May 6, 1919; July 10, 1919; June 1, 1923; July 2, 1923; November 10, 1923; March 15, 1924; April 20, 1924; May 4, 1924.

B 153
To Grace Hart Crane and Elizabeth Belden Hart
Phrases, sentences, and paragraphs from previously unpublished letters are included in Unterecker, *Voyager,* 1969. The page number of *Voyager* is in parentheses following the date of each letter: January 2, 1917 (54, 57, 58, and 62); June 1, 1923 (303); July 19, 1923 (308); November 21, 1926 (329); December 30, 1923 (341); April 3, 1924 (350); October 14, 1924 (369); October 25, 1924 (379); November 9, 1924 (372); March 13, 1925 (380 and 392); April 21, 1925 (373); May 2, 1925 (373); January 17, 1926 (424). The following letters are published in whole or part in Thomas S. W. Lewis, "Hart Crane and His Mother: A Correspondence," *Salmagundi,* 9 (Spring 1969), 61–87: January 2, 1917; October 26, 1917; January 19, 1924.

B 154
To Caresse Crosby
A portion of a letter dated March 16, 1930, appears in Sy Kahn, "Hart Crane and Harry Crosby: A Transit of Poets," *Journal of Modern Literature,* 1, first issue (1970), 45–56.

B 155
To Caresse Crosby
Phrases, sentences, and paragraphs from previously unpublished letters are included in Unterecker, *Voyager,* 1969. The page number of *Voyager* is in parentheses following the date of each letter: April 19, 1929 (589); April 25, 1929 (589 and 591); September 30, 1929 (602); January 2, 1930 (612); January 15, 1930 (617); January 22, 1930 (614); February 8, 1930 (613 and 617); March 16, 1930 (374 and 627); April 19, 1930 (627); April 19, 1930 (615); April 25, 1929 (591); May 13, 1930 (613 and 627); January 9, 1931 (639 and 645); April 5, 1931 (652).

B 156
To Harry Crosby
Phrases, sentences, and paragraphs from previously unpublished letters are included in Unterecker, *Voyager,* 1969. The page number of *Voyager* is in parentheses following the date of each letter: undated (1929?) (588); February 17, 1929 (584); February 24, 1929 (585); May 6, 1929 (593); May 16, 1929 (591 and 593); June 7, 1929 (595); July 23, 1929 (600).

B 157
To Harry and Caresse Crosby
Phrases, sentences, and paragraphs from previously unpublished letters are included in Unterecker, *Voyager*, 1969. The page number of *Voyager* is in parentheses following the date of each letter: March 13, 1929 (587); April 13, 1929 (589); April 22, 1929 (591); July 1, 1929 (595); October 17, 1929 (604); October 29, 1929 (605); October 30, 1929 (605).

B 158
To Zell Hart Deming
A portion of an undated letter (1928) appears in Philip Horton, *Hart Crane: The Life of an American Poet*. New York: W. W. Norton, Inc., 1937, p. 244.

B 159
To Lorna Dietz
Phrases, sentences, and paragraphs from previously unpublished letters are included in Unterecker, *Voyager*, 1969. The page number of *Voyager* is in parentheses following the date of each letter: June 17, 1930 (629); July 17, 1930 (631); April 7, 1931 (652 and 653).

B 160
To Waldo Frank
A portion of the letter dated February 17, 1929, previously unpublished, appears in Unterecker, *Voyager*, 1969, p. 583.

B 161
To Solomon Grunberg
Phrases, sentences, and paragraphs from previously unpublished letters are included in Unterecker, *Voyager*, 1969. The page number of *Voyager* is in parentheses following the date of each letter: January 21, 1931 (644); February 25, 1931 (642 and 646); May 9, 1931 (666); September 24, 1931 (694); October 20, 1931 (678, 682, 684, 686, 687, 688, 697, and 703).

B 162
To Charles Harris
"Letters of Hart Crane," *The Free Lance*, 5 (First Half, 1960), 17–24. Includes five letters: May 11, 1923; February 20, 1926; November 30, 1926; undated; undated.

B 163
To Charles Harris

Phrases, sentences, and paragraphs from previously unpublished letters are included in Unterecker, *Voyager*, 1969. The page number of *Voyager* is in parentheses following the date of each letter: April 19, 1923 (249, 290, and 294); December 21, 1925 (422).

B 164
To Elizabeth Belden Hart
Phrases, sentences, and paragraphs from previously unpublished letters are included in Unterecker, *Voyager*, 1969. The page number of *Voyager* is in parentheses following the date of each letter: January 7, 1916 (42, 55, 60, 61); July 19, 1923 (303); November 10, 1923 (328); October 24, 1925 (409); December 29, 1925 (419); March 18, 1926 (428); May 25, 1926 (441); July 29, 1926 (449); February 28, 1927 (471). The letter of January 7, 1917, is published in full in Thomas S. W. Lewis, "Hart Crane and His Mother: A Correspondence," *Salmagundi*, 9 (Spring 1969), 66.

B 165
To jh (Jane Heap)
The Little Review, 9 (Autumn 1922), 39. To Jane Heap, one of the editors of *The Little Review*, regarding *Secession*.

B 166
To Helen and Griswold Hurlbert
A portion of the letter dated September 20, 1931, previously unpublished, appears in Unterecker, *Voyager*, 1969, p. 690.

B 167
To Otto Kahn
"Two Letters on *The Bridge*," *Hound and Horn*, 7 (July–September 1934), 677–682. Includes a letter from Kahn to Mrs. Crane as well. Horton, *Hart Crane*, 1937, prints the September 12, 1927, letter. *The Letters*, 1952, nos. 235 and 289. *Complete Poems*, 1966, reprints the letter of September 12, 1927.

B 168
To Richard Laukhauff
A portion of the letter dated February 10, 1932, previously unpublished, appears in Unterecker, *Voyager*, 1969. p. 729.

B 169
To Samuel Loveman
"Last Letters of Hart Crane: With a Commentary on the Poet and the Man," *Literary America*, 1 (September 1934), 7–14.

The commentary is by Rita Joyce Lipton. *The Letters*, 1952, nos. 358, 369, 378, and 398.

B 170
To Samuel Loveman
Phrases, sentences, and paragraphs from previously unpublished letters are included in Unterecker, *Voyager*, 1969. The page number of *Voyager* is in parentheses following the date of each letter: Christmas-New Year's, 1926 (467); December 1, 1927 (519); December 25, 1928 (576); January 8, 1929 (577); February 19, 1929 (584); October 22, 1929 (604); November 11, 1929 (606); June 1, 1930 (629); June 8, 1930 (629); July 12, 1930 (630); September 7, 1930 (632); February 16, 1931 (641 and 645); August 14, 1931 (682).

B 171
To N. Byron Madden
A portion of the letter dated April 20, 1932, previously unpublished, appears in Unterecker, *Voyager*, 1969, p. 748.

B 172
To Henry Allen Moe
Phrases, sentences, and paragraphs from previously unpublished letters are included in Unterecker, *Voyager*, 1969. The page number of *Voyager* is in parentheses following the date of each letter: March 4, 1931 (646); May 11, 1931 (665); July 8, 1931 (667); July 22, 1931 (680).

B 173
To Harriet Monroe
First published in *Poetry*, 29 (October 1926), 35–39. An exchange of correspondence with Harriet Monroe, the editor of *Poetry*, regarding "At Melville's Tomb," which appeared in the same issue. Horton, *Hart Crane*, 1937. *Twice a Year*, 12–13 (1945), 439–446. Brom Weber, *Hart Crane*. New York: The Bodley Press, 1948. *Complete Poems*, 1966.

B 174
To Gorham Munson
First published in Horton, *Hart Crane*, 1937, pp. 341–345. Weber, *Hart Crane*, 1948. *The Letters*, 1952, no. 234. *Complete Poems*, 1966.

B 175
To Gorham Munson
Phrases, sentences, and paragraphs from previously unpub-

lished letters are included in Unterecker, *Voyager,* 1969. The
page number of *Voyager* is in parentheses following the date
of each letter: April 1, 1920 (166 and 169); January 31, 1921
(189); March 12, 1921 (189 and 213); April 11, 1921 (212); June
24, 1921 (206 and 214); June 29, 1921 (207); August 21, 1921
(213 and 215); January 2, 1922 (225); February 11, 1922 (231
and 249); May 25, 1922 (228); October 12, 1922 (257); October
18 or October 19, 1923 (313, 320, and 314); October 24, 1923
(321); November 31, 1923 (333); August 6, 1925 (396).

B 176
To *The Pagan*
First published in *The Pagan,* 1 (October 1916), 43. Crane's
first published prose. Horton, *Hart Crane,* 1937, p. 32.

B 177
To Margaret Robson
A portion of the letter dated July 29, 1931, previously unpub-
lished, appears in Unterecker, *Voyager,* 1969, pp. 679 and 681.

B 178
To Selden Rodman
Phrases, sentences, and paragraphs from previously unpublished letters are included in Unterecker, *Voyager,* 1969. The
page number of *Voyager* is in parentheses following the date of
each letter: March 10, 1930 (614); November 12, 1930 (636);
May 23, 1931 (666).

B 179
To Charlotte Rychtarik
Phrases, sentences, and paragraphs from previously unpublished letters are included in Unterecker, *Voyager,* 1969. The
page number of *Voyager* is in parentheses following the date
of the letter: April 23, 1923 (296); July 9, 1923 (303).

B 180
To Richard Rychtarik
Phrases, sentences, and paragraphs from previously unpublished letters are included in Unterecker, *Voyager,* 1969. The
page number of *Voyager* is in parentheses following the date of
each letter: April 4, 1923 (296); May 24, 1923 (291).

B 181
To Richard and Charlotte Rychtarik
Phrases, sentences, and paragraphs from previously unpub-

lished letters are included in Unterecker, *Voyager*, 1969. The page number of *Voyager* is in parentheses following the date of each letter: March 30, 1923 (292); April 4, 1923 (288 and 289); May 30, 1923 (299); November 16, 1923 (327 and 329); April 15, 1924 (354); November 18, 1924 (366); October 14, 1925 (309); September 26, 1925 (401); October 22, 1925 (408); December 31, 1925 (421); April 11, 1926 (432); August 14, 1926 (451); July 9, 1927 (507 and 508); May 4, 1931 (662); May 14, 1931 (665); March 1, 1932 (732); April 20, 1932 (749).

B 182
To Carl Schmitt
Portions of three letters appear in Horton, *Hart Crane*, 1937. The page number of *Hart Crane* is in parentheses following the date of each letter: Probably November 1916 (36); probably 1917 (53); probably November 1917 (55). Unterecker reports that all of Carl Schmitt's letters from Crane were stolen from him in Italy just before the beginning of World War II. A portion of the November, 1916, letter to Schmitt is reprinted in *The Poet's Vocation: Selections of Letters from Hölderin, Rimbaud, & Hart Crane*, edited and translated by William Burford and Christopher Middleton. Austin, Texas: University of Texas Press and Humanities Research Center, University of Texas, 1968. Includes, as well, parts of the following letters previously published in *The Letters*: 3, 4, 24, 39, 66, 78, 85, 101, 123, 126, 135, 137, 138, 141, 142, 148, 149, 154, 171, 173, 182, 183, 191, 192, 234, 248, 260. All are published in part only and selected for publication by the editors because they illustrate the relationship between the poet's art and his life. "The letters selected here may be read as a testament to three great expeditions in art and in life, always perilous for the absolutist, but always necessary to him."

B 183
To Isadore and Helen Schneider
A portion of the letter dated December 15, 1927, previously unpublished, appears in Unterecker, *Voyager*, 1969, pp. 519 and 520.

B 184
To Eyler Simpson
Phrases, sentences, and paragraphs from previously unpublished letters are included in Unterecker, *Voyager*, 1969. The page number of *Voyager* is in parentheses following the date of each letter: April 12, 1931 (656); May 1, 1931 (661).

B 185
To Mrs. T. W. Simpson
A portion of the letter dated December 7, 1931, appears in Unterecker, *Voyager,* 1969, pp. 678 and 706.

B 186
To Tom Smith
A portion of the letter dated May 11, 1931, previously unpublished, appears in Unterecker, *Voyager,* 1969, p. 665.

B 187
To William Sommer
A portion of the letter dated October 11, 1923, previously unpublished, appears in Unterecker, *Voyager,* 1969, p. 319.

B 188
To Alfred Stieglitz
Phrases, sentences, and paragraphs from previously unpublished letters are included in Unterecker, *Voyager,* 1969. The page number of *Voyager* is in parentheses following the date of each letter: December 27, 1926 (466); February 17, 1929 (583).

B 189
To Allen Tate
"Lettere Inedite e Poesie Scelte," *Inventario,* 1 (Fall–Winter 1946–1947), 89–97. Includes translations into Italian of "North Labrador," "Passage," "Legend," "Voyages V," and "Voyages VI." *The Letters,* 1952, nos. 98, 100, and 343. *Complete Poems,* 1966, prints no. 343.

B 190
To Allen Tate
Phrases, sentences, and paragraphs from previously unpublished letters are included in Unterecker, *Voyager,* 1969. The page number of *Voyages* is in parentheses following the date of each letter: April 16, 1923 (294); an unsent letter, probably 1926, undated on Mizzen Top Hotel stationery (434); March 25, 1927 (481); April 23, 1927 (490); December 14, 1929 (610).

B 191
To Jean Toomer
Phrases, sentences, and paragraphs from previously unpublished letters are included in Unterecker, *Voyager,* 1969. The page number of *Voyager* is in parentheses following the date of each letter: November 23, 1923 (331); May 28, 1924 (361); June

16, 1924 (361, 362, and 375); August 19, 1924 (362); November 4, 1923 (325, 326, 327, and 328); November 23, 1923 (325 and 329).

B 192
To Wilbur Underwood
Phrases, sentences, and paragraphs from previously unpublished letters are included in Unterecker, *Voyager,* 1969. The page number of *Voyager* is in parentheses following the date of each letter: January 31, 1921 (190); September 2, 1922 (274); September 19, 1922 (274); May 19, 1923 (295); November 3, 1923 (325); January 11, 1927 (469); March 21, 1927 (476); May 4, 1927 (491); May 12, 1927 (495); May 23, 1927 (495); June 6, 1927 (497); July 15, 1927 (506); August 17, 1927 (506); October, 1927 (515); November 7, 1927 (517); November 11, 1927 (518).

B 193
To Louis Untermeyer
A portion of the letter dated July 24, 1931, previously unpublished, appears in Unterecker, *Voyager,* 1969. p. 680.

B 194
To Charmian Von Wiegand
Phrases, sentences, and paragraphs from previously unpublished letters are included in Unterecker, *Voyager,* 1969. The page number of *Voyager* is in parentheses following the date of each letter: August 9, 1928 (551); August 20, 1928 (554 and 556).

B 195
To William Carlos Williams
Phrases, sentences, and paragraphs from previously unpublished letters are included in Unterecker, *Voyager,* 1969. The page number of *Voyager* is in parentheses following the date of each letter: September 15, 1922 (268); September 19, 1922 (269); September 16, 1928 (559).

B 196
To Yvor Winters
First published in part in Horton, *Hart Crane,* 1937, pp. 224–226. *The Letters,* 1952, no. 285. *Complete Poems,* 1966.

B 197
To Mrs. William Wright

A portion of the letter dated December 7, 1931, previously un-published, appears in Unterecker, *Voyager,* 1969, p. 708.

B 198
To William Wright
Phrases, sentences, and paragraphs from previously unpublished letters are included in Unterecker, *Voyager,* 1969. The page number of *Voyager* is in parentheses following the date of the letter: July 7, 1918 (113); August 9, 1918 (116); February 9, 1919 (121); April 10, 1919 (137); December 14, 1919 (152, 154, 155, and 162); September 28, 1920 (179); October 2, 1921 (218); January 25, 1922 (225); February 13, 1922 (231); June 11, 1922 (242); July 12, 1922 (246); August 25, 1922 (257); May 25, 1926 (442); November 15, 1926 (473); March 11, 1927 (474); Feb-ruary 13, 1929 (582); April 29, 1930 (626, 627, and 633); De-cember 16, 1930 (637 and 640); January 14, 1931 (643 and 644); April 23, 1931 (652).

B 199
To Morton Dauwen Zabel
A portion of the letter dated July 9, 1931, previously unpub-lished, appears in Unterecker, *Voyager,* 1969, p. 677.

C. Drawings

SLATER BROWN. BY HART CRANE

(C 2)

C 1
Brown, Susan Jenkins, a pencil drawing of

Susan Jenkins Brown, *Robber Rocks: Letters and Memories of Hart Crane*. Middletown, Connecticut: Wesleyan University Press, 1969.

C 2
Brown, William Slater, a caricature of

The Dial, 86 (February 1929), 123.

C 3
Frank, Waldo, a sketch of

S4N, (Fall 1923), frontispiece.

C 4
Rosenfeld, Paul, a creative impression of

Entitled "Annointment of Our Well Dressed Critic or Why Waste the Eggs?"—Three Dimensional Vista, by Hart Crane *The Little Review*, 9 (Winter 1922), 23.

D. Translations

ARABIC

D 1
Khal, Yussef, ed. *Diwan Asher Al Amerik*. Beirut: Dai Majallat
Sher, 1958.
Contains "Voyages I," "Voyages II," and "The Broken Tower."
Arabic only.

FRENCH

D 2
Bosquet, Alain, ed. *Anthologie de la Poésie Américaine*. Paris:
Librairie Stock, Delamain et Boutelleau, 1956.
Contains "Indiana," "Cape Hatteras" (in part), and "Cutty Sark."
English and French on facing pages.

D 3
Brown, John, ed. *Panorama de la Littérature Contemporaine
Aux Etats-Unis*. Paris: Librairie Gallimard, 1954.
Contains "The River" (in part). French and English on facing
pages.

D 4
Les Ecrivains et Poètes des Etats-Unis d'Amérique. Paris:
Editions de la Révue Fontaine, 1945.
Contains "And Bees of Paradise" and "Forgetfulness," trans-
lated by Jean Wahl. French only.

D 5
Ginestier, Paul, ed. *Les Meilleurs Poèmes Anglais et Américans
d'Aujourd'hui*. Paris: Société d'Edition d'Enseignement Su-
périeur, 1958.
Contains "Chaplinesque." English and French on facing pages.

133

D 6

Guiguet, Jean, ed. *Au Pont de Brooklyn et Autres Poèmes de Hart Crane*. Paris: M. J. Minard Lettres Modernes, 1965.
Contains "To Brooklyn Bridge," "Ave Maria," "The Harbor Dawn," "Southern Cross," "At Melville's Tomb," "Voyages II," "Voyages IV," "Voyages VI," and "The Broken Tower." English and French on facing pages.

D 7

Jolas, Eugene, ed. *Anthologie de la Nouvelle Poésie Américaine*. Paris: Simon Kra, 1928.
Contains "O Carib Isle!" French only.

D 8

LeBreton, Maurice, ed. *Anthologie de la Poésie Américaine Contemporaine*. Paris: Les Editions Denoël, 1948.
Contains "Praise for an Urn" and "The River" (abridged). English and French on facing pages.

GERMAN

D 9

Leisegang, Dieter, trans. *Moment Fugue*. Darmstadt: Das Neueste Gedicht, Band 21, J. G. Bläschke Verlag, 1968.
Contains "October–November," "Postscript," "Fear," "Carrier Letter," and "Moment Fugue." English and German on facing pages.

D 10

Uhlmann, Joachim, trans. *Weisse Bauten*. Berlin: Das Neue Lot, Band 4, Karl Henssel Verlag, 1960.
A translation of *White Buildings,* containing presumably the 1926 table of contents. We have been unable to locate and examine a copy of this book.

ITALIAN

D 11

Baldini, Gabriele, ed. *Poeti Americani, 1662–1945*. Torino: Francesco De Silva, 1949.

Contains "My Grandmother's Love Letters" and "Chaplinesque."
English and Italian on facing pages.

D 12
Izzo, Carlo, ed. *Poesia Americana del '900.* Parma: Guanda,
1963.
Includes "Praise for an Urn," "My Grandmother's Love Let-
ters," "Royal Palm," "The Harbor Dawn," "Black Tambourine,"
"At Melville's Tomb," "Chaplinesque," and "The Hurricane."
English and Italian on facing pages.

D 13
"Léttere Inédite e Poesie Scelte," *Inventario,* 1 (Fall–Winter
1946–1947), 89–97.
Contains "North Labrador," "Passage," "Legend," "Voyages V,"
and "Voyages VI." Italian only.

D 14
Rizzardi, Alfredo, ed. *Lirici Americani.* Caltanissetta-Roma:
Edizioni Salvatore Sciascia, 1955.
Contains "Garden Abstract" and "North Labrador." English and
Italian on facing pages.

D 15
Sanesi, Roberto, ed. *Poeti Americani.* Milano: Feltrinelli Editore, 1958.
Contains "Voyages I," "Voyages III," "To Brooklyn Bridge,"
"Van Winkle," "Indiana," "Cutty Sark," "Cape Hatteras" (in
part). English and Italian on facing pages. Includes a brief essay on Crane.

D 16
Sanesi, Roberto, ed. *Poeti Americani da E. A. Robinson a W. S.
Merwin (1900–1956).* Milano: Feltrinelli Editore, 1958.
Contains "Voyages I," "Voyages III," "To Brooklyn Bridge,"
"Van Winkle," "Indiana," "Cutty Sark," and "Cape Hatteras"
(abridged). English and Italian on facing pages.

D 17
Sanesi, Roberto, ed. *Il Ponte e Altre Poesie.* Parma: Guanda,
1967.
Contains *The Bridge* and all the poems in *White Buildings.* English and Italian on facing pages.

NORWEGIAN

D 18
Brekke, Paal, ed. *Amerikansk Lyrikk*. Oslo: H. Aschehoug & Co. (Nygaard), 1957.
Contains "Chaplinesque," "Garden Abstract," "North Labrador," "Voyages I," "Voyages II," and "Voyages III." Norwegian only. Also includes a twenty-six-line excerpt from "Cape Hatteras" in English only.

SPANISH

D 19
Bishop, John Peale, and Tate, Allen, eds. *Antología de Escritores Contemporáneos de Los Estados Unidos*. Santiago, Chile: Editorio Nascimento, 1944.
Contains "To Brooklyn Bridge" and "Voyages II." English and Spanish on facing pages.

D 20
Brown, John, ed. *Panorama de la Literatura Norteamericana Contemporánea*. Madrid: Ediciones Guadarrama, S. L., 1956.
Contains "The River" (in part). English and Spanish on facing pages.

D 21
Florit, Eugenio, ed. *Antología de la Poesía Norteamericana Contemporánea*. Washington D.C.: Union Panamericana, 1955.
Contains "At Melville's Tomb." English and Spanish on facing pages.

D 22
Manent, M., ed. *La Poesía Inglésa: Los Contemporáneos*. Barcelona: Ediciones Lauro, 1948.
Contains "North Labrador," "Royal Palm," and "The Hurricane." English and Spanish on facing pages.

D 23
Salvador Novo, ed. *101 Poemas: Antología Bilingüe de la Poesía Norteamericana Moderna*. Mexico: Editorial Letras, S. A., 1965.
Contains "The Hurricane," "Voyages II," and "Repose of Rivers" English and Spanish on facing pages.

TURKISH

D 24
Ball, Robert H., ed. *Cagdas Amerikan Siirleti*. Ankara: Sairler Yapragi, 1956.
Contains "Black Tambourine" and "Voyages II." Turkish only.

YIDDISH

D 25
Licht, Michel, ed. *Modern American Poetry*. Buenos Aires: Julio Kaufman, 1954.
Contains "Poster." Yiddish only.

E. Adaptations

E 1
Dance drama adaptation of *The Bridge*
The Bennington School of Arts produced *The Bridge,* performed with individual actors, choral speaking, dance, and music as an exercise in the use of theater space. The production was directed by Arch Lauterer. An account of the production appears in *Theatre Arts,* 24 (July 1940), 501–503. Three photographs of the scene design are included. The entire production was done without omitting a single line or changing the order of a word in the sections of the poem.

E 2
The Poems of Hart Crane, read by Tennessee Williams. Caedmon Records. TC1206.
Includes the following poems: "To Brooklyn Bridge," "Powhatan's Daughter," "Cutty Sark," "Three Songs," "Legend," "My Grandmother's Love Letters," "Praise for an Urn," "Voyages III," "Voyages V," "Key West," "O Carib Isle!" "The Hurricane," "The Broken Tower." "Phantom Bark," and "Eternity."

E 3
" '*Voyage*' (*Hart Crane*)" *a Musical Composition for Voice and Piano,* by Elliott Carter. South Hadley, Massachusetts, and Northampton, Massachusetts: The Valley Music Press, Mount Holyoke College, and Smith College, 1945.
A musical setting for "Voyages III" with a commentary by the composer.

F. Doubtful Attributions

F 1

"Chanson"

First published in *Aesthete, 1925* (January 1925), 27, Weber, *Hart Crane*, 1948. The authorship of the poem is in dispute. In the periodical the name *Walter S. Hankel* is appended to the poem. Hankel was the fictitious editor of *Aesthete, 1925.* Weber tentatively suggested that Crane might have been the author of the poem, since the copy of this issue of *Aesthete, 1925* in the Princeton University Library was presented to Princeton by Allen Tate with the name *Hart Crane* written across the lines of the poem. Susan Jenkins Brown made the following statement: "Bill's [Slater Brown] contribution to *Aesthete, 1925* was a 'Chanson' signed by the name of our fictitious editor, Walter S. Hankel. Before it got into print, 'Chanson' bore a few traces of other hands. In it Bill took a friendly poke at Gorham Munson's occasional lapses into profundities . . ." ("Hart Crane: The End of the Harvest," *The Southern Review*, 4 [Autumn 1968], 965). She asserted directly that Weber's attribution of "Chanson" to Crane is incorrect. In addition, Weber did not include it in his 1966 edition of *The Complete Poems*, and Allen Tate wrote the following to us on April 21, 1970: "I'm afraid I can't help you. I could easily have been wrong in attributing 'Chanson' to Hart Crane. So I suspect that we must accept Mrs. Brown's word for its authorship."

F 2

Supplement to the Plain Dealer Correspondent

In an envelope addressed to George Bryan and postmarked Cleveland, January 6, 1919, Hart Crane sent a copy of a four-page burlesque newspaper, with a typescript note at the top of the first page which reads: "Dear George:—Here is something to read on a dull, lonely evening that beats the movies. Hart." The front page reads as follows: 'SUPPLEMENT TO THE | PLAIN DEALER CORRESPONDENT | [double rule] | December, 1917. | [single rule] | GORE RUNS LIKE WATER AS BOLD | BANDITS, AFTER MAD CHASE, ARE | THWARTED

145

IN THE NICK OF TIME' followed by text. The copy of this burlesque paper with Crane's note at the top is now in the Rare Book Room of the Ohio State University Libraries. There is no clear evidence that Crane was the sole or joint author of this burlesque, and it is entirely possible that he had no hand in it at all; furthermore, we find nothing in the style of the burlesque which seems to be clearly indicative of Crane's hand. The fact that Crane did send the paper to his friend suggests, however, that he might have had some hand in it, and Hugh C. Atkinson, Assistant Director of Libraries at Ohio State, has ventured the opinion that internal stylistic evidence "seems to point to Crane as at least a participating author."[1]

---

1. In a letter to the compilers of December 30, 1970.

Appendices / Index

Appendix I

A Chronology of Crane's Life

1899 Harold Hart Crane, born July 21, in Garrettsville, Ohio, the only child of Clarence A. Crane and Grace Hart Crane. During the next four years the family lived in Warren, Ohio.

1908 Parents separated temporarily, Mrs. Crane going to a sanitarium in the East and Mr. Crane to Chicago. Sent to live with his grandmother in Cleveland. Later, the three were united in Cleveland, where his father organized The Crane Company, a chain of retail candy shops.

1913 Enrolled in East High School in Cleveland and began to write verse. Began his friendship with William Wright.

1915 Took a trip with his mother to his grandmother's plantation on the Isle of Pines in the West Indies. After returning to Cleveland, met Mrs. William Vaughn Moody, the poet's widow, who encouraged his interest in poetry. Visited Elbert Hubbard at East Aurora, New York.

1916 Had first poem, "C 33," published in *Bruno's Weekly*. Toured the West with his mother. After his parents were divorced, dropped out of school, took a job in Cleveland in a picture store, and finally left for New York, where he was supposed to study for college and spend time writing.

1917 A young painter and family friend from Warren, Carl Schmitt, looked after him in New York. Took a room at 308 East Fifteenth Street. Met Joseph Kling, editor of *The Pagan;* Padraic and Mary Colum; Alfred Kreymborg; and Maxwell Bodenheim. After his mother's divorce, she came to New York and he moved to her apartment at 44 Gramercy Park. Struck up a friendship with Claire Spencer, daughter of his mother's friend. Mrs.

Crane returned to Cleveland planning to remarry Mr. Crane. Mr. Crane called off the remarriage, and Mrs. Crane spent some time in New York with Hart again, finally returning to Cleveland. Moved to 25 East Eleventh Street. Used "Hart Crane" as his name for the first time in a published piece.

1918   Became an associate editor of *The Pagan*. Returned to Cleveland and worked for a few months tightening bolts on machine parts in a munitions plant. Tried to enlist for military service. After being turned down because of age, worked as a riveter in the Lake Erie Shipyard. Was drafted, but influenza epidemic forestalled his induction. After the war ended, worked for three months as a reporter for the Cleveland *Plain Dealer*.

1919   Returned to New York and took rooms at 307 West Seventieth Street with Alexander Baltzly. Resigned as associate editor of *The Pagan*. Became a close friend of Gorham Munson. Took a position as advertising manager of *The Little Review* and moved to 24 East Sixteenth Street, a garret above *The Little Review* offices. Met Matthew Josephson. Harrison and Claire Spencer Smith helped him with meals and money. Resigned from *The Little Review* and took a job with Rheinthal and Newman, an agency for the reproduction of Maxfield Parrish paintings. Left New York for Akron, Ohio, to clerk in one of his father's candy stores. Began to correspond with Sherwood Anderson and started his friendship with H. W. Minns, the photographer.

1920   Worked in his father's candy business in Cleveland and went to Washington, D.C. as a candy salesman.

1921   Quit the job with his father and searched unsuccessfully for employment in Cleveland.

1922   Wrote advertising copy for Corday & Gross, an advertising agency in Cleveland. Met William Sommers, William Lescaze, Charles Harris, and Richard and Charlotte Rychtarik. Gorham Munson visited in Cleveland, having just returned from Europe.

1923   Returned to New York and lived temporarily with the Gorham Munsons at 4 Grove Street. Met Waldo Frank,

Jean Toomer, Kenneth Burke, William Slater Brown, E. E. Cummings, Eugene O'Neill, James Light, and Susan Jenkins (Brown). Took a job in the statistical department of J. Walter Thompson advertising agency. Stayed for a short while with Slater Brown and then moved to 45 Grove Street. Resigned from Thompson advertising agency to devote full time to his writing. Moved to Woodstock, New York, with Slater Brown and Edward Nagle.

1924   Returned to New York with the Greenberg manuscripts given him by William Murrel Fisher. Unemployed, moved from room to room throughout March and April. Malcolm Cowley got him a job with Sweet's Catalogue Service, Inc. Moved to 110 Columbia Heights, Brooklyn, to the room once occupied by Roebling, the architect of the Brooklyn Bridge. A young sailor, the subject of "Voyages," lived with him. Met Allen Tate.

1925   Resigned from Sweet's and went to Patterson, New York, with the Slater Browns. Bought twenty acres of land near them with $200 lent him by the Rychtariks. Returned to his room at Columbia Heights in New York and was unemployed. Received $1,000 from Otto Kahn, with a promise of $1,000 more in two installments, to enable him to work on *The Bridge*. Went to Patterson, New York, to live with Allen Tate and Caroline Gordon.

1926   Quarreled with the Tates and returned to New York, where he joined his mother. With Waldo Frank sailed for the Isle of Pines. Frank left at the end of May. Remained until a hurricane destroyed his house. Completed much of *The Bridge*. Returned to New York and Patterson. *White Buildings* was published by Liveright.

1927   After visiting Cleveland, moved to Patterson. Received another $500 from Otto Kahn in addition to the $2,000 he had already received. Went to California as traveling secretary to Herbert Wise for five months. Met Yvor Winters.

1928   Resigned his position with Wise and joined his mother and grandmother in Hollywood. Returned to New York after a quarrel with his mother and spent two months in Patterson. Worked off and on at various jobs. Met

Walker Evans. His grandmother died, leaving him a legacy of $5,000. A quarrel with his mother over payment of the bequest precipitated their final estrangement. Shortly before December left for England and the Continent with the money from his grandmother's bequest.

1929   Spent seven months abroad. In London met Robert Graves and Paul Robeson. In Paris Met Harry and Careese Crosby, who agreed to bring out a special edition of *The Bridge*. Was arrested, imprisoned, and fined for a public disturbance and fighting. Returned to New York in July and finished *The Bridge*.

1930   The Liveright edition of *The Bridge* was published in April, three months after The Black Sun Press edition was printed in Paris.

1931   Lived for a few months with his father in Chagrin Falls, Ohio. In March was awarded a Guggenheim Fellowship and returned to New York. In April sailed for Mexico and settled in Mixcoac, a community that included Katherine Anne Porter, the painter David Alfaro Siqueiros, and Peggy Baird. Father died; returned to Chagrin Falls for the funeral. After staying a few weeks, returned to Mixcoac and visited William Spratling. Lived with Peggy Baird, former wife of Malcolm Cowley.

1932   Wrote "The Broken Tower." Sailed from Vera Cruz on the S.S. *Orizaba*, bound for New York. Shortly before noon on April 26, leapt from the stern of the ship and was lost at sea.

1933   *The Collected Poems of Hart Crane* was published.

Appendix II

A Chronology of the Publication
of Crane's Poems

"C 33"	September 1916
"October–November"	November 1916
"The Hive"	March 1917
"Annunciations"	April 1917
"Fear"	April 1917
"Echoes"	October 1917
"The Bathers"	December 1917
"In Shadow"	December 1917
"Modern Craft"	January 1918
"Carmen de Boheme"	March 1918
"Carrier Letter"	April 1918
"Postscript"	April 1918
"Forgetfulness"	August 1918
"To Portapovitch"	March 1919
"Interior"	November 1919
"Legende"	November 1919
"North Labrador"	November 1919
"My Grandmother's Love Letters"	April 1920
"Garden Abstract"	September 1920
"Black Tambourine"	June 1921
"Porphyro in Akron"	August 1921
"Pastorale"	October 1921
"A Persuasion"	October 1921
"Chaplinesque"	December 1921
"Locutions Des Pierrots"	May 1922
"Praise for an Urn"	June 1922
"The Great Western Plains"	August 1922
"Voyages I"	January 1923
"America's Plutonic Ecstasies"	May 1923
"Stark Major"	August 1923
"Possessions"	Spring 1924
"Recitative"	Spring 1924

"Interludium"	July 1924
"For the Marriage of Faustus and Helen"	Winter 1924
"Chanson" (?)	January 1925
"Legend"	September 1925
"Paraphrase"	September 1925
"Lachrymae Christi"	December 1925
"Voyages II"	Spring 1926
"Voyages III"	Spring 1926
"Voyages V"	Spring 1926
"Voyages VI"	Spring 1926
"The Wine Menagerie"	May 1926
"Repose of Rivers"	September 1926
"At Melville's Tomb"	October 1926
White Buildings	December 1926
"Passage"	1926
"March"	March 1927
"National Winter Garden"	April 1927
"O Carib Isle!"	April 1927
"Southern Cross"	April 1927
"Virginia"	April 1927
"Cutty Sark"	June 1927
"The Harbor Dawn"	June 1927
"To Brooklyn Bridge"	June 1927
"To Emily Dickinson"	June 1927
"Old Song"	August 1927
"The Dance"	October 1927
"Van Winkle"	October 1927
"The Tunnel"	November 1927
"Bacardi Spreads the Eagle's Wings"	December 1927
"The Hurricane"	December 1927
"The Idiot"	December 1927
"Island Quarry"	December 1927
"Royal Palm"	December 1927
"Ave Maria"	1927
"The Air Plant"	February 1928
"The Mermen"	September 1928
"The River"	1928
"Moment Fugue"	February 1929
"A Name for All"	April 1929
"The Mango Tree"	November 1929
The Bridge	January 1930
"Cape Hatteras"	March 1930

"Indiana"	April 1930
"To the Cloud Juggler"	June 1930
"The Broken Tower"	June 1932
"By Nilus Once I Knew . . ."	January 1933
"The Circumstance"	January 1933
"Enrich My Resignation"	January 1933
"Havana Rose"	January 1933
"Imperator Victus"	January 1933
"Phantom Bark"	January 1933
"A Postscript"	January 1933
"Purgatorio"	January 1933
"Reliquary"	January 1933
"Reply"	January 1933
"The Sad Indian"	January 1933
"The Visible, the Untrue"	January 1933
"—And Bees of Paradise"	February 1933
"Eternity"	February 1933
"The Return"	February 1933
"A Traveler Born"	February 1933
Collected Poems	March 1933
"To Shakespeare"	April 1933
"In a Court"	September 1934
Collected Poems (Boriswood)	November 1938
"Belle Isle"	1948
"The Bridge of Estador"	1948
"Children Dancing"	1948
"Episode of Hands"	1948
"Euclid Avenue"	1948
"Lenses"	1948
"The Masters"	1948
"Mirror of Narcissus"	1948
"Oyster"	1948
"The Pillar and the Post"	1948
"A Placement"	1948
"Sonnet"	1948
"To Liberty"	1948
"To the Empress Josephine's Statue"	1948
Complete Poems	January 1958
"The Moth that God Made Blind"	November 1960
"The Alert Pillow"	1964

Seven Lyrics	January 1966
"With a Photograph to Zell, Now Bound for Spain"	February 1966
"With a Photograph to Zell, Now Bound for Spain"	May 1966
Complete Poems	September 1966
"Happy Feast Days"	December 1966
[Untitled]	1969
"Of an Evening Pulling Off a Little Experience (with the english language)"	1969

Appendix III

Periodicals in Which Crane's Poetry and Prose First Appeared

(The number of appearances is given within parentheses.)

Aesthete (?)
American Weave
Broom
Bruno's Bohemia
Bruno's Weekly
The Calendar (London) (6)
Columbia Library Columns (2)
Contempo
The Criterion
The Dial (10)
The Double Dealer (4)
The Futitive (4)
Gargoyle (2)
larus: The Celestial Visitor
Literary America
Literary Digest (3)
The Little Review (10)
The Measure
The Modernist (3)
The Modern School
The Nation
The New Republic (8)
The Pagan (16)
Poetry: A Magazine of Verse (17)
Saturday Review of Literature
Secession (2)
S4N (2)
transition (12)

Index

159